Dear Ryan

The Story of a Sad Little Girl Who Smiled a Lot

Dee Stephens

DEAR RYAN
The Story of a Sad Little Girl Who Smiled a Lot

To my priest
who guided and inspired

and to the guardian angels
that watch over us

When I laid my eyes on you,
I could swear I saw God,
Smiling back at me,
Like I did when I was a child.

"Here I am," I whisper
"I am ready to love you."

"Here he is." He says.
His heart is ready for you.

PREFACE

Dear Ryan,

I missed you today at the Thanksgiving dinner. But I am glad you were not here. There are things that I am glad you do not see, and this Thanksgiving dinner with the family is one of them.

I planned the perfect menu for weeks. It looked exactly as I planned it in my head. The table was set beautifully and the perfect hors d'oeuvres were ready for serving. It was going to be wonderful because this has always been my favorite holiday. Everyone would sit around smiling and laughing. The food would be great. This would be the year finally; that a family celebration would be perfect! And then, here's what happened:

First, your cousin Sue, who lives in another state, called and said she is pregnant. No, she is not married, just pregnant.

Your Uncle Jim arrived with his fourth wife who is divorcing him because of his drinking. They came in separate cars.

Lynn, your oldest cousin, arrived next. She quit college last year, to do cocaine instead. She was going to be a pediatric neurologist.

We all sat down to watch some movie before dinner, but the DVD player didn't work. We only had two options at that point – to stare at each other or to find a way to make conversation. Lynn made the choice. She tried to talk to her dad; I mean, really talk to him. She did not begin with the weather but went straight to the real issues. Your Uncle Jim was never good with those things, so Lynn's attempt never went anywhere. Every subject was off limits, including his weight loss and his hair style. Desperate for some substantial conversation with her father whom she never sees, she began the outburst of the day: "I don't know who my father is and he won't talk to me," she said sadly. "For years I have tried to get to know him, but he won't let me." She sobbed and went outside. Your Uncle Jim cannot ever seem to handle these kinds of situations, so he got mad at her for crying and left. Then, his wife left. It all happened so fast.

I was left in the room wondering what to do. The turkey was still cooking but no one was left to eat it. I stood frozen in the middle of the room wondering what happened to my perfect Thanksgiving.

Three hours later, everyone came back, but no one talked to each other at all. The silence was unbearably painful, and I had no words to say that would help the situation. I planned the whole dinner well and I was sure that the food would turn out really good, but the turkey was dry, the dressing was gummy, and the potatoes were lumpy. The food just became a reflection of everything else that happened. The contentment of our family has long been dry, the richness of our lives that I have always longed for has turned from bland to gummy and any possible stronghold that could keep us together as one happy family has been broken, if not, lumpier than those potatoes at the table. Everyone left as soon as the awful dinner was over. Thanksgiving left a bad taste in my mouth. I threw out the leftover food with sadness and regret.

The day was a disaster, and I am always surprised. I always look forward to it with hopes that it would be the best Thanksgiving ever. At the end of the day, I turn off the lights feeling let down and sorry for myself. There is not much to be thankful for about my family, even on Thanksgiving Day.

Ryan, this is our family. This is how we spend not only Thanksgivings but every holiday. They are always filled with dread and drama. You are still young now so I do not know if you actually get the big picture and I hope to God you don't, it would harm you. I hope and pray that you grow up spending better Thanksgivings with your family. I wish our family could give you wonderful memories that you will cherish for the rest of your life, memories that you would go back to with fondness and true thanksgiving. I think these are ordinary dreams of an ordinary grandmother to every special grandson like you. You deserve to have good memories, Ryan, memories which you can share with your children someday. But those good memories will happen only when you are able to make the decision to make them yourself. You can make good memories now, even as you deal with the challenges of being surrounded by dysfunction and the absence of many positive things that can empower you to be the good man that you can become. That is why I think that you are now at a special time of your life, my dear Ryan. You are just beginning this process called living, growing and learning what life is all about. You have a chance to have a different life, different from the one that many in our family know sadly, so well. And I want to be there for you, somehow, in this different path that I am offering you to take – the path of a good life, away from misery and any form of bondage.

This is why I thought of writing this book. This is a book for you from me. I hope it will guide or inspire you in breaking the ugly cycle that surrounds our lives, and have wonderful holidays with your family someday. I am writing this to you in case I am not around when you grow into the wonderful man that I know you will become, so that even then, you can go back to the pages of my own life, and hopefully understand the hard lessons that I learned along the way. God has blessed you with wonderful gifts and has blessed me with the time that I have been able to spend with you. I want to contribute to the good that I hope your life can become.

But you are already so good! I look at you as a little boy and I ask myself if you will be able to remember how good you are now. I hope you do, and I hope that this book can help you rekindle some of the things that I see in you now.

Even as a little baby, you amazed me. You always smiled and never cried, even when your diaper needed to be changed.

I loved holding you close and feeling you breathe. Even when you started to crawl and walk, never once did you touch something that you shouldn't. You were the perfect child from the very beginning.

Then you started to laugh. What a special laugh you had. It was not just a child's smile, it was a belly laugh. I loved hearing you laugh and it was so easy to make you laugh. You loved to be tickled. We had lots of tickle brushes that I saved from my makeup, and we had the super duper tickle brush (A computer cleaning brush) that we tried to get to first because it gave the best tickle. One time, we lay on my bed and just tickled each other until we couldn't laugh anymore.

When you began to talk, you called water *agua*! How did you know that was the Spanish word for water? No one ever taught you that word!

Every time you came to my house, which was never often enough, I stopped doing everything because I knew how valuable our time was and how fleeting the time would be until you grew up.

The times when we played together were the happiest times of my life, from hide-and-go-seek in my house (you would shout

out for me to give you a clue after I hid) to playing castle, which was your favorite thing to do. The castle didn't do anything and cost $1 at a garage sale. You liked to pretend and you were so good at shooting down the men with the ball after I lined them up.

One evening, while we were having your favorite chicken and spinach noodles for dinner, you were being silly so I said sternly, "Ryan, sit down and eat you dinner right now!" but you just laughed.
I said, "Ryan, I mean it!!!" even more sternly, but you laughed harder.
"What makes you think I don't mean it?" I asked you angrily.
"It's just a roar," you said with a big smile on your face.
"What's a roar?"
"You know, it's what lions do to scare you."
You were only four. Where did you get that idea?

You met John the director of the food bank once and you met my priest Father Mike twice, yet every time you said your prayers, you prayed for both of them. What could you see?

One day we were driving and I said, "Ryan, I am so blessed!"
You replied, "That's because Father Mike and your friend John are praying for you."
"How do you know that"? I said.
"Because they are your friends and that's what friends do."
You were four but you had the wisdom of a century-old sage.

I also remember the time when you ran upstairs to your dad's room and filled both of your hands with change from the change bottle. Your dad finally asked what you were doing after the fifth trip. When he went downstairs, you showed him an envelope filled with change. ???
"Ryan, what were you going to do with that money?' he asked.
"I am going to give it to God, because it is God's money."

You had only been to church three times.

Ryan, yesterday on the way to my house, out of the blue, you said,
"I have been praying since I was born, even before I knew words."
"How did you do that?"
"In my head, I remember being in my crib and looking through the bars praying to God."
Last night, when I tucked you in, you blessed Father Mike twenty times.
"Why did you bless him so much?" I asked.
"Because I love him so much." You have only seen him twice.

Sometimes when I tucked you in at my house after we laid in bed feeding grapes to each other and watching America's Funniest Home Videos, you would tell me that you loved me more than Saturn (which was your favorite planet) and I would tell you I loved you more than all of the planets. Then, you would tell me you loved me more than the planets, and all of the stars, and the sun and the moon. And you know what? I knew you meant it.

Then there were the 752 learning games that we played. I never let you give up, even when you thought you could not do the task; I always knew you could do it. I believed in you with all my heart.

But you know the most special thing of all? You called me Macca! No matter how much we tried to correct it and get you to call me Gram, you would not change it. You gave me my very own special grandmother name and for that I am grateful.

For all these times we spent together, you have seen me laugh, giggle, and enjoy living. You have only seen me happy, but I can assure you it has not always been like that. The story you will read will be sad and painful but it is important for you to know who I am. Hopefully you will understand that you can overcome any obstacle in life and still be joyful and happy like I am today. If I can go through what I have gone through and still be happy, anyone can be happy.

I want you to know that every second, every minute, every hour that I spent with you was truly a blessing from God. Thank you for being Ryan. The joy that you have given me makes up for all the pain.

Love you, miss you,

Macca

CHAPTER 1
THE AWFUL CHILDHOOD

CHILD OF WAR

The year 1943 was a time of war. Americans were uniting to make airplane parts and boat parts, anything that they could do to help America prevail over the conflicting world powers. Everybody was passionate about it. The war was the immediate subject of every conversation. There was no need to ask. People lined up to volunteer to do something, including the women.

Claire Elizabeth Blodgett was a yeoman second class for the US Navy Reserve in Dallas. It would be hard to tell just by looking at her that she could be an asset at all to the service. After all, she was very petite at her five foot frame. She had the all-American look that defined that era. Her beautiful blue eyes spoke of charms. She could stare at you like she was looking straight into your brain. Her short light brown hair matched her eyes perfectly and, when she smiled, all that you could notice was her prominent set of teeth that protruded a bit forward. Nothing about her spelled anything like Navy yeoman but, then again, she might just have wanted to be away from home, if being with her mother who was divorced from her father could be called home at all. There is always that time when one just knows that it's time to leave. Twenty-three years was long enough to not know anything about the world, and be confined to being with mother and going to church every Sunday. Enlisting in the Navy and being part of this great reality called World War II must not have been such a bad idea.

Claire Elizabeth Blodgett, my real mom

Claire took the leap of faith and entered into the service. It was like being set free. In a way, she became a changed woman and, in no time at all, she was fighting a war of her own. I don't know much more about her story but during this time in the service, she got drunk at a party one night and had sex with an Italian man. She had no idea who he was.

But that was all it took for her to get pregnant. He said he wanted to marry her, but she said no. Then he was gone and she was all alone. Because she was pregnant, she got discharged from the service. "Thanks for your service," they said, and she was asked to pack her bags immediately. She was ready to go home thinking everything would be just fine, until she actually called home.

"Mom, I have great news," she announced, trying to muster some excitement in her voice. "I have been discharged early from the service. I will be coming home soon."
"I have not heard from you for a long time," her mom said.
"That's because I have been afraid to tell you that I am going to have a baby," Claire said, trying to be nonchalant about it. It was a point of no return.

"What?! What is wrong with you Claire? What were you thinking?! You will not bring a baby into my house. Get rid of it." The voice was stern, and final. She knew her mother. There was no negotiating, no ifs, ands or buts. She had to get rid of the baby, or she could not go home.
"What am I supposed to do, Mom?"
"Give the baby away or else, don't talk to me again." Her voice sounded even more final, sterner than the Navy telling her that her work with the war was over.
"Mom, please do not make me do this too. I have always tried to do whatever you wanted but, please, don't make me give my baby away."
For Claire, the real war just began.

Mildred Hessey Blodgett, Claire's mom

* * * * * * * * * *

Florence Nightingale Hospital was as cold as the December breeze outside. The hallways and the lobbies were all well decorated with Christmas ornaments. The big day of the coming of God into the world was just a couple of days ago, but there was nothing to celebrate within the walls of Claires hospital room. There was no compassion left for Claire there.

They did not even sew her wounds back after her delivery, when they found out that she was giving birth to an illegitimate child. They kicked her out of there the same day she gave birth to her baby girl. There was nowhere to go. She could probably relate to Joseph and Mary looking for a place to stay but she knew there was nothing immaculate about her, so to even think of that was blasphemy in her mind. God would have every reason to abandon her, and it felt He had. No one was there for her at all.

But then, she remembered her friend Lillian, the only friend that she could think of who might be willing to take her in. She wasted no time and painfully walked straight to her doorstep. She asked to have a place to stay until she was well enough to go home.

It hurt when she opened her eyes the next day. She must have slept very long. The light coming from the small but clean room of her friend's house was blinding her. Lillian deserved to know everything that was going on and Claire had to tell the whole story so she could get it out of her mind and have a much needed peaceful sleep. The baby was still sleeping by her side. She looked peaceful and content; thank God she was too small, and unaware of what was going on. She had to tell Lillian everything.

"Just give her to me," Lillian said unhesitatingly, as she poured a glass of milk into a plastic cup. "I am so glad nothing happened to the baby when you were forced out of the hospital for giving birth to an illegitimate child. How can they send you away like that? That's not really safe, you know."

"Thanks, Lillian…" She looked at her friend who was willing to open the doors of her home for her at the most difficult time of her life. Lillian's life seemed so well put together, while hers was without question a big mess. She looked at the little angel sleeping beside her one more time. Claire thought Lillian would do a better job taking care of her baby girl. "I can't take care of her; I need my mom..." she whispered, like talking to herself. No one knows how hard or how simple it was for Claire and Lillian, but the verbal transfer took place. That day, the little girl became Lillian's daughter.

That little girl was me.

Claire gave me away because she needed a mom. She was twenty-four. She did not think that I needed a mom; I was five days old. When she left me with Lillian, she went straight back to her mother, but soon after that, an infection developed from the complications of her delivery. She had to be hospitalized for two months. The doctor told her that the infection caused so much damage in her system that she would not be able to have any children. Four months later, her mom died of a disease caused by alcoholism at the age of forty-five. For Claire, life turned out to be one very sad irony.

As for me, there was never an adoption or foster care. My blank birth certificate was impounded for being an illegitimate child. No one knew I existed. No one ever told me that Lillian was not my real mom and that the man she was married to at the time was not my real dad. I presumed in my growing up years that they were my parents. But deep within, I always questioned why something inside did not settle well about Lillian.

Although Joe was already her third husband, Lillian never had children of her own. She could not have kids because she had been raped when she was thirteen years old, which permanently damaged her reproductive system. She was thirty-five when she took me and somewhere deep within, she must have had some longing to be a mother.

THE STATES OF TEXAS

COUNTY OF TARRANT

  WHEREAS, I, CLAIRE ELIZABETH BLODGETT, am the mother of an infant girl baby born December 27, 1943 at Florence Nightengale Hospital at Dallas, Texas, and being desirious of obtaining for such child a fit and suitable home and to place her in custofy of someone who will care for, support and educate such child, and whereas Joseph Francis Stephens and wife, Lillian Anna Stephens are willing to perform such service in behalf of such child.

  Therefore, I, the said CLAIRE ELIZABETH BLODGETT, in consideration of the above do hereby deliver such child into their possession and assign to them all of my maternal care and custody thereof. I hereby consent for adoption of this child after six months, or when the Court sees fit, from date hereof.

  Witness my hand, this the 19th day of January, A.D., 1944.

<u>Claire Elizabeth Blodgett</u>
CLAIRE ELIZABETH BLODGETT

  SWORN TO and subscribed before me, this 19th day of January, A.D., 1944.

<u>Juanita M. Powledge</u>
JUANITA M. POWLEDGE,
  Notary Public, Tarrant County,
  Texas.

My commission expires 6/1/45.

8

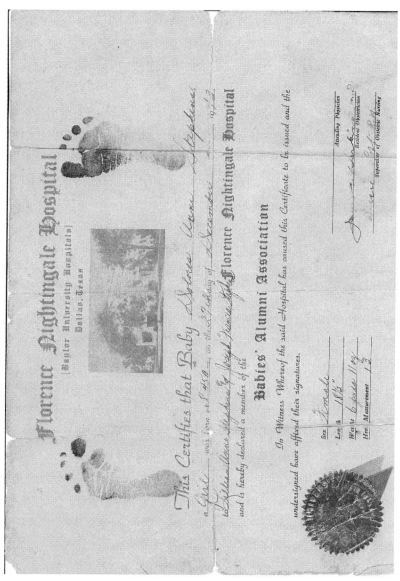

This was the certificate of birth from Florence Nightingale Hospital. The attending physician refused to sign it. The names of the child and the parents were filled in later on by Claire, after she gave me to Lillian.

Joe was happy to have a little baby in the house. It also gave him some sense of fatherhood. He took care of the baby like it was his own. He had a big smile whenever he carried me around and gave me bottled milk. He always looked at me with the kind of loving tenderness that a father would have. But he was not going to be around to be my father. Joe was dying of tuberculosis. He loved me as his baby, and made Lillian promise to raise me Catholic because he was Catholic. There was no way to say no to the wish of a dying man. I remember going to see him in the hospital. I could only talk to him through the window. He died when I was two. I thought my dad had died.

Suddenly, Lillian was alone again, without a man by her side. It was like isolation. She was alone. Alone to face the world, handle the problems and to fulfill the responsibilities. I was there, suddenly an added burden, someone she had to raise on her own, and she could not give me back. I think from this point on, she always resented my presence and I was always afraid being around her because I somehow sensed that resentment. I remember that whenever I woke up crying because I was having bad dreams, she would yell at me for bothering her. My crib was a witness of my early pains. I must have known in the confines of my little world that I was not wanted.

Lillian started having an affair with a married man named Lather. Everyone called him Lock. He later became the fourth of Lillian's seven husbands. Lock would be my stepfather for the next thirty years. I was never allowed to be alone with or talk to him. Lillian always thought I would grow up and take her husband away because she had married her stepfather at one time.

Lillian was Lutheran, Lock was Baptist, and I would be raised Catholic. I went to Catholic school and attended masses at a

Catholic Church, all by myself. I was the only one in my family that attended church. It was the only time I felt safe.

CHILD OF SORROW

Childhood is a very important time in every human being's life. Many things about our childhood form the basic patterns of our living and help shape our personality. That is why I think that this time of your life is very special, my dear Ryan. You are only a child once, but what you see now has such a strong impact on what you can become.

I remember crying a lot when I was a little girl. My mother always accused me of lying, stealing, and talking back. It seemed like every time I did anything or said anything, I was doing something that was wrong and irritating to her.

When we were out, if I asked for something in the store she would hit me so hard that I would fly across the aisle. No one ever tried to help me. That was a completely different time and place altogether. The rod was not spared and I was not spoiled.

At home, if I ever did anything wrong, she would hit me with her strong back hand and I would cry. She would then hit me even harder for crying and continue hitting me until I stopped.

"Stop crying!" she would yell while hitting me with her hand. I would try my best to not cry, like I was drowning and trying to breathe at the same time. I would find myself in a corner sobbing and wondering what I had done to deserve being hit.

Once, I felt desperate because my body was in so much pain. I saw Lock while mother was hitting me over and over, I called out for help.

Lock, my stepfather, was going to play a crucial role in my life... He chose to not be there for me when I needed him, but even in my abandonment, I seemed to always choose to smile. You can see that in this picture...

"Dad, help me..."
"Leave me out of it," he said, and walked away. I looked at him as my father but he obviously did not look at me as his daughter, simply the daughter of his wife. Even then, I felt abandoned. To this day, I can feel that abandonment and it has caused tremendous problems with my relationships through the years. I never trusted anyone to help me if I needed it. It did

not take long for me to learn not to cry when hit. I didn't cry again until I was thirty-four.

By now Ryan, I hope you are beginning to understand why I never allowed you to say "sorry" at my house. When you were three and came to my house, you must have said sorry thirty times a day. I paid careful attention and finally figured it out. You were saying it in advance, so no one would yell at you in case you did something wrong.

You never did anything wrong, Ryan. Even now, if you spill something you get that fearful look in your eyes, and say" are you mad"? No Ryan, I never got mad.

When your dad was not around, I heard your mom say "You are so stupid, Ryan."
She also called you an idiot once, in front of me.
"Bad Ryan, bad," she would say, and then your sister started saying it too. I tried to tell your dad about it but he said it was not true.

Ryan, I just wanted to pick you up and take you to my house and never give you back. It was like hearing my mom all over again, and I did not want you to hurt the way I had.

I understand that that was the way your mom was raised and she didn't mean it, but it hurt your soul. I felt your pain and tried to always be positive with you and affirm how wonderful I know you are. You have a kind, loving heart and a gentle soul. You are the most caring person that I have ever met. When people around you tell you things that make you think less of yourself, it is most likely about them, not about you. Believe that you are good and that you can do great and wonderful things with your life. Then you will be empowered and will not be afraid to do well.

Lillian had a contract to go to Hollywood but had an accident that prevented her from going. I knew her as my mother, but I also felt that something wasn't quite right from the start...

Almost every day my mom told me how useless I was. She said I would never have anything and God would punish me. I would get what I deserved. My mom was punishing me and I thought God was too. I didn't stand a chance.

I grew up with the idea, that if anything went wrong, it was God punishing me but I hadn't even done anything wrong yet. I thought if God was a loving God, I could have a better life. It has taken me a lifetime to understand free will.

I always made good grades, hoping my mom would approve. She never did. I was enthusiastic and always believed this time would be different. One day, I proudly presented her with my report card and she tore it up and threw it on the floor. From then on, I forged her signature and she never asked how I was doing or where the report cards were.

* * * * * * * * *

My grandmother babysat me and these were happy times in my life because she was the only person that was ever sweet and loving towards me. When I was with my grandmother, I always wished I never had to go home to my mom.

I liked going to grandma's house because she didn't yell or hit me. I would go there and make mud cookies and pretend to sell them. No toys. I never had anyone to play with. I spent a lot of time with my grandmother. She was nice to me and felt sorry for me. She would make wonderful meals for me. She made roast chicken and dressing, baked macaroni and cheese, and the best blackberry cobbler I have ever had. It nurtured my spirit! Maybe that is why good food is so important to me today, because it is connected to the few good memories that I have of being with someone that loved me. Grandma lived next door to a tavern. When the tavern moved, so did she. I remember thinking how strange that was. She didn't drive. I guess they really liked her because they made sure she had a house to rent near the tavern. She drank her beer everyday but I never saw her drink too much. She would always give me beer to make me sleep. I think she thought it would make me sleep better. It worked for her.

On Sunday she would take me to the tavern. Customers would give me money to play slot machines while she drank. I was a natural with the slot machines; I always won. I enjoyed listening to the sound of the coins rolling into the tray. It kept me from getting bored. It gave me something to enjoy inside the tavern. I saved the money that I won from those slot machines and never touched it. It was my own little investment and I treasured it very much.

My grandmother never forgave my mom for taking her husband away. I discovered it one day while I was looking through pictures. My grandmother told me what happened but we never talked about it again. It must have been very sad and painful to be betrayed by her own daughter. I just hope that somehow she found peace with it all because she was already a victim and to carry that burden of un-forgiveness would have made her life miserable. Maybe that's why she was going to the tavern, to drown her pain in beer.

She died when I was twelve at my house, in my bed, from cancer. Now I had no one.

ALWAYS SICK

I was very sickly as a child and, at times, I actually hoped against hope that it would at least get me some attention, or care. It never did.

I remember once I had a high fever. I had pus coming out of my eyes. My mom told me to take a bus to the doctor because she didn't want to take me. It was pneumonia; my temperature at the doctor was 105. I almost died, but I took the bus.

THE SAND CASTLE

We lived across the street from a beach in Galveston, Texas. To live in a small island of a big country like America is quite unique and special. Being so close to the water always gave me this sense of freedom and awe. So whenever my mom would let me, I would go to the beach. The beach was peaceful. I would listen to the waves splashing against the warm sand on my feet. I was always in awe of the fluffy clouds over the water and would pretend to see animals in the clouds. The hermit crabs trying to grab the coquina shells in the sand fascinated me. I would splash about in the shallow water and imagine a different life. I do not know how I knew it should be different because I had nothing to compare to, but I did. No one could hurt me at the beach.

The highlight was always to build a sandcastle. Not just any sand castle but one with moats, balconies, and rivers. I was happy in my castle. It was a place where I did not have to do anything to feel loved. In my sand castle, I was just loved, accepted and nurtured. I would pretend that I was a princess and a prince would come and rescue me from the horrible life I had. He never came.

That is why I always want to go to the pool to build sand castles, Ryan. They have always been a source of comfort. It will always be the place of my dreams.

CHILD LABOR

Whenever I was by the beach, I would stroll around looking for sea shells. Their shapes and colors fascinated me. I felt God designed these little shells just for me. I would go home with a bag full of shells and would look at each one of them like precious gems. When I stayed home sick, I would spend hours gluing the shells together, making all kinds of animals out of them. Over time, I made so many that my mom put them in the station wagon, took them down to the beach, and sold them for souvenirs. It proved to a big hit to tourists, she discovered, that she could actually make good money out of them.

So, I would have to continue making these. I was eventually making shell jewelry for Neiman Marcus, decorating purses with shells, and making animals for Woolworth's. I came home every day to work. I was only eight and continued to do this until I left home at seventeen. I did not know how much profit she was making but Mom paid me ten cents for an hour of work.

DREAMING OF CHRISTMAS

You always wondered why I made an issue about your big birthday parties and all of the Christmas presents and toys. Do you remember whenever you watched a commercial and saw a toy, you would say, "I want that!" and I would say, "Ryan, there are lots of kids in the world that don't have any toys, and you have too many already." I was one of those kids. I never had a toy and I only received one Christmas present in my entire childhood -- a bike when I was twelve, but I could only ride to the corner and back.

My mother started giving me money for Christmas to buy myself something when I was six but I never did. I would spend it on other people. I would buy her Midnight In Paris perfume, my dad a tie or hankies, and my aunt chocolate covered cherries, so I could eat them.

I never had a holiday dinner either. Because my mom had a souvenir shop, we had to be open 365 days a year. My mother was always afraid she would not have enough money. She was importing shells from all over the world and it grew into a big business because of me gluing shells together. To this day, I cannot stand crafts.

Lillian never cooked a meal, but for Christmas she would make delicious fruitcake, unlike any fruitcake you will ever have. I still cannot have Christmas without her fruitcake. Today, my friends look forward to it every year. It was the only thing she ever cooked. It is my Christmas and the only good memory I have ever had of that day.

We did have a little two foot Christmas tree once on top of the TV, but no presents, and definitely no joy. To this day, my Christmas tree and holiday dinners mean everything to me because I never had them. My children have never understood what it means for me. I want it to be special! I have tried to make it that way for my family. My granddaughter is the only one that understands how much it means to me. My sons (*yes, including your dad*) are oblivious.

LITTLE MISS COOK

I made all of my own food from the time I could reach the stove. My grandmother taught me how to cook so I could take care of myself. My dad usually cooked for myself and my mom because he owned a cafeteria, and he apparently knew what he was doing in the kitchen. I never saw my mom in the kitchen. They ate very strange things like mashed potatoes and buttermilk, scrambled eggs, and cow brains. I would sooner starve to death than eat that kind of food. We lived across the street from a grocery store so she would let me go buy my own food and make it myself. I do not remember ever sitting down with my family for dinner.

When my mom would try to make me eat okra and soft boiled eggs that my dad had cooked, I would throw up and she would beat me.

TWEEDLE DEE TWEEDLE DUM

My mother bought me a purple tweed coat once. It was beautiful. I was about eight or ten. There was an African American family that lived behind us. They had 13 kids. My mother was the most prejudice person I knew. I don't think she liked anyone, but she hated black people. I could not see color. All I saw was a little girl when I showed her the coat through the fence. She said that she did not have a coat so I gave her mine. It still had the price tags on it. I got beat for that but I never forgot how happy the little girl was to get the coat, that is, until I had to go get it back.

I still buy coats for the needy, and Ryan, I have given you a coat every birthday. I just want to make sure you are warm.

I recently asked if there were any families at church that did not have coats for their kids and I went and bought them some. When my granddaughter was living with me, I bought her three coats. To me, coats are very important and now there is no one to tell me that I cannot give them away. I didn't recognize this until now, but it is my rebellion towards my mom. I hope it is a good rebellion though because I would not have had the passion to do this if I did not feel so strongly about that memory in my childhood. Father Mike even said that maybe someday I will be the patron saint of coats and have a statue of me wearing a big coat to remind people of the joy that comes with giving.

ALONE WITH MYSELF

I was never allowed to have friends to play with, nor to be around other kids. My mother told me I would like their moms better than her. I'm sure I would have.

When I wasn't in school or working at her shop, I was alone in my room. It is amazing that I grew up with any social skills at all. I had no role models and everything that I think or feel today is based on my perception of how life should be. I observed other people, took a psychology class, and had years of personal counseling. I had no family and no one to tell me what was right or wrong. When I was raising my own kids, I wish I would have had someone to guide me.

This is my story and I'm sticking to it. It has a good ending but many years of molding. People think I am arrogant, tough, and aloof. This is what I project. But deep inside, I am scared that if they knew how much love I have and how soft I am inside, they might hurt me. Very few people have been allowed inside my heart. It is very hard for me to let people see who I am but, lately more and more people are seeing it, in spite of my cover.

Ryan you are one of those unique people that have a special spot in my heart because you want to be as close as you can get to me. You said no one gives better hugs. When you are tickling me and feeding me grapes, I feel God's presence. You have a way about you that makes me comfortable about being myself, as your grandmother, but also as someone whom you love and loves you very much. I think this is what love does. It makes someone feel at home so that they do not have to fear, or worry about not being accepted. All these many years, I have been searching for that home and you have given me a sense of it, even at your age. Now, it is not just me and God... I have you too, and some other very select friends that God has given me. I am grateful.

BEADS OF HOPE, ALTAR OF SORROW

Even in the midst of pain and sorrow, I still found a way to smile and laugh a lot as a child. Simple things had a way of bringing me joy. But the one thing that gave me the most joy was praying. The only real relief I had from the pain of my childhood was my rosary that I kept under my pillow. I would pray myself to sleep every night, thinking of happy thoughts with a smile on my face. I still have the same rosary and it is still under my pillow. Today, if I wake up during the night, I just touch it and say a prayer. It always brings me peace. The Rosary is a beautiful prayer because it helps me to think and focus on the life of Jesus and what God did for all of us. When I do not know what to say, it is good to use the words of the Angel Gabriel: "Hail Mary, full of grace, the Lord is with you..." Then, I can think of what God did through Mary. In God, nothing is impossible. When I think of that, even today, I can sleep peacefully. *I am so glad to know that you also love praying the Rosary. It brings me joy to watch you pray with your eyes closed, repeating the words of the Angel Gabriel. I know God has a special ear for children so I hope that you continue talking and keeping Him close to your heart.*

Having a constant presence of God was very good for me. So, I made an altar in my room. It had statues of Mary and Jesus. I got flowers from the florist down the street when they threw them out. I would dig through the dumpster and take the best ones for my altar. I prayed and prayed. I kept convincing myself that someone up there was listening to me, even if I could not see anyone or hear a voice talking back to me.

First Communion. I really believed in God. Who knew what that might have done for the rest of my life? It was the only peace I had in my heart.

GOD, WHERE ARE YOU?

I kept praying for a better life. I prayed for my mother and father. I prayed to feel happiness, instead of fear. I prayed to have peace and to feel loved.

But nothing changed. I felt like I was caught in a vicious circle. I could not understand why God had placed me in this horrible environment. I started feeling abandoned. If there really was a God, why did I have to suffer? I believed, I had faith, but it seemed hopeless. There was no one to talk to and nowhere to go.

I was twelve when I took a bottle of aspirin. I really wanted to make the pain stop. I could not distinguish what pain it was, if it was in my body, spirit, heart, or life. I just knew I was living in pain and I wanted it gone, even if it meant ending my life. I wanted to die but I only got sick. I never told anyone; after all, no one seemed to care.

I heard my mother calling out my name in the hallway. I didn't answer. She did not look for me. I just stayed sick until I could get up again. I always lived in darkness. I was not allowed to open the big wooden storm shutters in my room. I had to live in total darkness; I wanted to see the light. I used to try and peek through the shutters that mom had wired shut. This is why today, the only time I close the blinds is when I am changing clothes. I need to have light and to be able to see outside. There were nine bedrooms upstairs and I lived in the one farthest away from my mom. No one else lived upstairs with me. They used it for storage. Mother never went upstairs, except when she would measure my bath water to make sure I was not wasting water.

I now fill the tub to the top.

SELF CONTROL

The only time I can remember being even a little happy was in school. I was allowed to be with other people. I never told anyone about what was going on at my house because I thought everyone lived as I did.

I liked school. It was easy for me; I didn't need to study. I did well academically but behavior was a problem. On every report card, it said I needed self control because I could never be quiet. The nuns would distribute a blue or gold bow at the end of every semester. The gold and blue bows were given to the students that had good grades and were always behaved. The blue bow was for the students that just had good grades. I never got the gold bow because I was always misbehaving in class. Of course, I understand now. It was the only time I was allowed out of my room. I needed someone to talk to. I just couldn't stop visiting with my friends.

I always had something to say. I still do and no one has ever understood why I say what I think. No one ever told me I shouldn't.

The nuns at Ursuline Academy had their hands full. I had the principal, Mother Agnes, for my teacher once. She was one of the sternest looking women I have ever seen in my life. She was a big woman who never smiled and wore those wire-rimmed glasses that made her look even more intimidating. She always had a ruler in her hand to hit you with if you didn't behave. She always seemed to have her eyes on me because I was always trying to talk to someone, so she moved my desk into her office, adjoining the classroom. I looked into the classroom through the double doors but I still managed to get into a lot of trouble. My punishment, I had to stand on tiptoes with my nose on a dot on the blackboard. It was worth the punishment to be able to talk to someone.

Outside the classroom, I was always the boss. When we went to church as a class, sometimes I would pretend to faint, and they would let me go have breakfast with the priest because I told them that I could not fast; it made me dizzy. The girls in my class respected my power and would do whatever I told them to do. I even told them that if they saw the candle flicker, it was because they had sinned and they believed me! The candles always flickered, of course, and I could see them feeling guilty about themselves, if not just perplexed. I was always trying to entertain myself. Whenever I saw the rays of the sun beaming through the leaves of the trees, I would say, "God is coming down! Let us kneel. Everybody kneel!" And everyone would do it, solemnly. It was fun.

I formed some club that had no real purpose except for us to hang out and do fun, mischievous, harmless things. Everybody wanted to be part of it. I invented a game that if someone wanted to belong to the club, she had to go to a stranger's house, pretend to faint, get something to eat for herself, and have enough to share to the others. I would show them how to do it and then they would have to do it too. If I couldn't be the leader, I wouldn't play. For some reason they always let me be the leader. I think it is because I was the one that could think of silly things to do.

Every day I went past a bakery on my way to school. I would stop and get deliciously hot, greasy donuts on my way. After school, they sold ice cream. I would get a gooey marshmallow sundae with chocolate ice cream. This was my way of taking care of myself and trying to make myself feel good. It is one of the few good memories that I have of my childhood.

* * * * * * * * *

When I was in junior high, I got the lead in a play. I was so excited and worked very hard to get it exactly right. I told my mom, certain she would come to see me become a star. She would be so proud of me. She did not come.

THE GREAT ESCAPE

I spent a lot of time planning an escape from my own prison, "our house." The attempts I had in the past didn't work so I came up with a new plan.

When I was fourteen, my parents left and I decided to run away. I was locked in and could not go out through the front door but I could go into the backyard. We had an eight foot chain link fence with locks on the gates. I had nowhere to go, but I was willing to try anything.

I climbed the fence and, as I got to the top, they pulled into the driveway. I tried to jump over, but when I jumped, my jeans got caught on the top of the fence, and I was hanging upside down. It seems funny now, but I got a severe beating for it and was banished to my room, again.

THE DAY I FOUND OUT

When I was fifteen, I wanted a bathing suit because we lived near the beach.
I was standing on the stairs to my room. "Mom can I please have a new bathing suit because the other one is too small?"
"No!" Mom said emphatically.
"You're not my real mother; my real mother would buy me the bathing suit," I said angrily.

"No, I am not. Your mom didn't want you and I don't either," she said indifferently.

It felt like a bucketful of ice water was poured on my body. My world went upside-down. Questions rushed into my head all at once. What?! You're not my mom? Who is? I didn't know if I should be glad or sad. My real mom didn't want me and I was raised by a person that didn't want me either. I felt like someone had taken the air out of my body. I had always been sad but now I had no one that wanted me. That meant that the man that died was not my dad. No mom or dad. My grandmother was not even my real grandmother. I always knew my mom didn't like me or love me, but now I was alone with nowhere to go and no one that wanted me. I did not exist. I had no beginning.

I was broken; my soul was wounded. I didn't know I could hurt so badly. It just kept getting worse.

"No, I am not. Your mom didn't want you and I don't either." This one statement of Lillian's would control my life for years to come. I would go in search of someone or something that would make me whole again. For a long time, I felt I did not belong. But now that I heard it from the woman that I thought was my mother, I realized that I had really been standing in the midst of strangers. I was actually on my own. I had to face the world alone.

* * * * * * * * *

I decided the only way out of my house would be to quit school and earn enough money to take care of myself. The ninth grade was the last full year of my education.

When I told my mom that I wanted to quit school and go to cosmetology school, she thought that was a great idea. I'm not sure she ever went to school so education didn't matter. Besides, she wanted me gone as much as I wanted to go. I was fifteen when I told my teachers and they were shocked. I was in accelerated classes and making good grades. They said I was too smart to quit. My teachers said I needed an education to be successful in life. I told them that they made a mistake by putting me with all of the smart kids and I had to quit. All I had to do was bring a letter from home.

I had already investigated how long beauty school would take and it was only a six month class, so I thought I could make a ton of money, in a short time, and be out of the hell that I called home.

CHAPTER 2
LET THE GAMES BEGIN

PUTTING MY BET ON LIFE

Beauty school was going to be the answer to my prayers. They put me to work as soon as I got to the door. Beauty school was crazy because I realized that I was good at doing hair color but really sucked at hairstyles and haircuts.

One of my first days at work, I gave a young lady a perm. I rolled her hair in this solution that filled the room with the smell of pungent ammonia and waited for the instructor to check if I did it right. She didn't come. I started hearing clinking sounds into the bowl as the rods fell one by one with the hair still rolled around them. The lady was basically bald at the end of that session and I knew I was in big trouble.

One lady asked me to give her a short haircut so I started cutting from one side. I never seemed to be able to balance the length of her hair, so I kept cutting from one side to the other until she ended up with hair that was cut above her ears. She looked like a Martian. She was not happy but that's what you could get, if you went to a beauty school for a cheaper haircut, especially one that didn't train their students before putting them on the floor to work.

Being as outspoken as I was, when people handed me a picture and said, "I want to look like this," it was all I could do not to laugh and tell them it was hopeless. I didn't think this was going to work right from the beginning, but I finished it anyway.

Needless to say, it was becoming clearer to me that this beautician thing was not going to work, that is, if I wanted to stay alive. But I had to stick with the plan. I understand now how some people can have murderous thoughts about their hairdressers. I hated the work and was never good at it.

While doing beauty school, the beauty convention was coming to Galveston and I was chosen to model and be part of this bathing suit beauty contest. It was an exciting time for me. After the pageant was over, we had a fun party. There were so many beautiful people, nice people. I was very naïve in this new environment. An executive from Revlon came up to me and invited me for more drinks in his room and I followed, thinking how nice it was of him to invite me. We kept drinking and I was enjoying my time getting drunk in his suite. He asked me how old I was, so I said I was sixteen. Immediately, he asked my phone number and called my dad to come and get me. No one ever mentioned it. I never knew why. It was my first time getting drunk but would not be my last.

Now that I had my beautician's license, I went to work in a shop. I knew I was not going to last. It was hard work and I was not making enough to even buy clothes. In no time, I was saying goodbye to being a beautician, to the pungent smell of ammonia, and to the bickering women who were never satisfied with their hairstyles. It was time for a new plan.

THE PERFECT PLAN

I kept brainstorming in my head and suddenly it came to me. How can I permanently leave home and never have to go back again? GET MARRIED! That had to be the perfect solution and all I needed to do was find someone to marry.

My hometown was a Coast Guard base, and a Navy base so it was not hard to find men. There were a lot to choose from, but I had no idea how to have a good relationship. I thought you just got married and lived happily ever after. That is what I had read. My mother and I never had "THE TALK." The only thing she ever told me was that you could get pregnant by kissing. Many years later, I asked her why she told me that and she said she thought if I didn't kiss I wouldn't do anything else. I told her I had done everything but!

Ryan, since no one explained anything to me about relationships, this is what I would say today. It took me all of my life to figure it out on my own. I think this will help you so you will not make the same mistakes I had to make to learn these things:

Be friends first. Love yourself; you cannot give something you do not have.

Be able to take care of yourself; never be completely dependent on someone to take care of all of your needs, emotional or otherwise.

Get your education first; without it, you will not be able to provide for your family.

Do not base everything on looks; it's what's inside that matters. Looks will change. The inside will only get better. I have ended relationships that had potential because I did not like the person's nose. It is ridiculous and I am not proud of those choices.

Get to know someone for at least a year. Watch for loving kindness, toward kids and animals. Remember they might someday be the mother of your children. This will show you their heart and soul.
Try and find out who they really are by observing their relationships with others, especially their family. This is probably how they will treat you.

Do not want to change someone. Love someone for who they are, not for who you want them to be.

Listen to what they are saying about past relationships. Who are they blaming? Are they accepting any responsibility for the failure? For many years, when I heard men say how awful their past relationships were, I would think, "That was her; I could love him more." Listen; don't hear what you want to hear.

Trust. If you have insecurities about the relationship, look at yourself not the other person.

Respect each other. Do not tolerate, even for a minute, someone who puts you down or tries to make you feel inferior. This will never stop. Don't defend who you are.

Laugh; if you can laugh, you can enjoy each other.

Have a faith you can share. This will help get you over the rough spots, and there will be many.

I did not know one of these things. My life was trial and a lot of error. Having knowledge of healthy relationships could not have prevented my decision to marry. I had no other option, but it certainly would have prevented future failures.

THE GUY WITH A CHEVY

I do not remember how I met Bill, the first boy, but I remember thinking he was gorgeous. He was tall, dark, and handsome like I had read about in romance books. He had a beautiful smile and dark, piercing eyes that I felt looked into my soul. He was nice, and he treated me with the respect that I wasn't getting at home. I was desperate for affection and respect. I thought I was in love, but I probably would have loved anyone that treated me nice. He was nineteen, had a job as a mechanic, and (the best part) a new 1959 white Chevrolet convertible. My kind of guy! One day, he came to pick me up. He pulled up on the lawn and drove up to the door. When my friends saw the car, I felt better than they were because I had an older boyfriend and he had enough money to buy a really nice car. I wanted them to be jealous. We had so much fun, the only real fun I had ever had. We slow danced to the Platters, holding each other close, looking into each other's eyes. This was heaven. One day, after six months, Bill looked at me with those piercing eyes and said, "I love you. Will you marry me?" "Yea!" (My plan was working!) I was very excited.

There was a little problem: he robbed a grocery store to get enough money to marry me. He got sent to prison. When I went to see him, Bill said, "I love you so much. I didn't mean to get into trouble, but I couldn't stand living without you and I could not make enough money fast enough."

"I promise I will wait for you forever," I said. I think I waited a week.

My mother said he would never have anything. He now owns a ski lodge in Vail.

I don't remember the next one. I just remember going to pick out the ring. I remember that I didn't like him at all, so I broke up and gave back the ring.

This was taking too long, I was already seventeen.

I met Larry in a bowling alley. It was LIKE at first sight. He was THE ONE. He was tall, thin, had beautiful eyes, and had a beautiful smile. Apparently I did not have a lot of qualifications.

He was Canadian French and had a beautiful olive complexion that never required sun tan lotion.

He was friendly, warm, and romantic. Every time I saw him, he had a gift or flowers for me. My heart was melting. I had never met anyone like him. I liked him immediately, and he made me laugh. We had so much fun. He was in the Coast Guard and told me he wanted to be a court reporter when his time was up. I thought he could provide a nice life for me and the six children that I wanted.

We saw each other every day for two weeks and then he asked me to marry him. He was four years older than me and I thought he knew a lot more about life than I did. He came from a good family and didn't seem to have any of the struggles that I had. I did not tell him anything about my home or family and he didn't ask.

"Is today too soon?" I thought. I wanted out of my house as soon as possible. I can't imagine what his family must have thought. They were 1200 miles away.

If you ever need someone to plan a wedding in a short time, I'm the person for the job.

I wanted a big wedding because it would be my first and last. I sent out invitations, bought my wedding dress, ordered flowers, reserved the church, and planned the hotel reception.

We were married twenty-nine days from the day we met at Sacred Heart Cathedral, in a beautiful ceremony. I planned everything and paid for it with money that I won at the slot machines I played when grandma took me to the bars. I must

36

have been planning it that way all along. It was a nice wedding and I was sure this was the answer to my prayers.

To get even with my mom for being so prejudice, I invited a black person to my wedding. She couldn't do anything about it; I was married!

My mother and his mother lived 1,200 miles apart and never spoke to each other, but wound up with the exact same dress, the same color, and the same color accessories. Strange things like this usually happened to me, things that did not happen to other people.

I was seventeen and he was twenty-one. We were going to have a great life. I was not capable of having a relationship with a flea, but I was certain this would work. Like almost every teenager, I knew it all!

* * * * * * * * *

Just last night, I was on the phone with Sue, my nineteen-year-old granddaughter, talking about her life. She met a guy in a club, had a one-night stand, and got pregnant.
"I was nineteen and pregnant too," I said. "It is very difficult to care for a child, so what are your plans?"
"I've thought of everything, I don't need your advice. I know how to care for my child," she retorted. She is two months pregnant but not married. She is living with her grandfather, until he finds out. Then, she plans to go on welfare. Yes, that's her plan.
"I raised two children without child support or welfare. Please find a way to provide for yourself and your child."
"You are just being negative and not supportive. I know what I am doing. I've thought of everything." She said.

I can't tell you how many times I thought that same thing when I was her age. The difference is I didn't have a family, no one to help me or give me advice. I could help her and be supportive, if she would let me.

* * * * * * * * *

Ryan, listen to your elders. They can help you. They have lived the hard part already. They really do know. Keep an open mind and don't be stubborn. We can all learn from other people. Do not ever think you know it all, at least listen. God has blessed me with the ability to ask for and try to follow advice. I had no skills on my own and have always listened to what people say. This is very important in my life. Everyone should ask and listen.

Larry, my new husband, had back surgery. When he did, his heart and lungs stopped, causing him to have epilepsy, so he was discharged from the Coast Guard. We moved away from the Gulf Coast to the Midwest to be near his family. I did not like the hot, humid weather anyway and the farther away from home I could get, the better.

I was so glad he was out of the Coast Guard. Now we could start our family. After we had been married a year, I got pregnant. I was eighteen and had a lot of problems with the pregnancy. I lost the baby (girl) at five months. My husband was more upset than I was. I knew it was for the best. The placenta grew, but the baby didn't. I always wanted to have six kids. Six weeks later, I got pregnant again. This time I delivered a healthy baby boy.

A baby was what I had wanted all of my life. I could love this child the way I had always prayed to have love for myself. I knew what I didn't get. I could make up for all of it by pouring my love into my baby. I had an instinct but no skills. I had never even seen a baby, except at the store. I had never had a doll. Now, I had a living, breathing real baby doll to take care of. Now what do I do?

I didn't know how to hold him or change his diaper. I was scared. I needed help. One day I called his doctor and said, "He won't stop crying." She said, "I don't hear him now." "That's because I'm holding him." "You don't have a problem," and hung up.

I was desperate. I called my mom. She sent the cleaning lady to help me. I was not surprised. Why would I expect her to start caring? Besides that, she knew nothing about raising kids.

He was so beautiful, bald head and all. He was perfect. I was convinced he would have a wonderful loving mom, dad, and someday beautiful brothers and sisters. So at nineteen, I had a husband and a baby boy with no parenting or family skills. Everything seemed fine.

CHAPTER 3
THE BEGINNINGS OF A BUMPY ROAD

TRAILERS, BLACKOUTS AND THE ACCORDION

Larry and I lived in a trailer park. I know, don't laugh. I trained myself not to have an accent because I was from the south living in a trailer park. My father-in-law bought us the trailer so we could get a start and have something of our own. The trailer was eight feet wide and thirty feet long. It consisted of a living room, dining area, kitchen, two bedrooms, and a bathroom. It was not air-conditioned so it was like living in a small tin can. I would take long walks to stay cool. I hated the trailer. I wanted an apartment. I was used to living in darkness, but now I had a brand new experience, living in a small, hot tin can.

My son, your Uncle Jim, was born on the hottest day of the year in August, and we had to live in what seemed to be 150 degrees every day. I could only lay him in the bassinet and pray for cool weather.

I did not drink for the first three years of my marriage. One day while walking my son to the office to do laundry; a man that lived across from the office asked me to come and have a cocktail while I was waiting for my laundry. Wow, I didn't know you could drink in the daytime. I had never had hard liquor. He worked nights and was home days. This was great. Drinking in the daytime made me feel completely free of responsibility. I loved it. I didn't feel guilty and would sneak out to do laundry to drink. My husband had no idea. After all, I wasn't involved with this man; I was only having a good time. Drinking with him was fun. Marriage was boring. I longed for excitement.

I went home to stand up for my best friend's wedding. I do not remember where it was, the church or the reception, because I drank the whole time I was there. I would not have remembered the wedding, if it had not been for the pictures. This was my first time away from my husband and child and I loved the freedom from all of the responsibility.

Being married and having a child was not making the pain from my childhood go away. My husband was nice, my child was beautiful, but I was not happy. The memories of abuse and rejection were causing constant emotional pain and drinking was the only thing that would mask it temporally. I never meant to get drunk or even a little high; I just wanted to have one drink. I called it my "recess from reality." I would think this every time I drank. I would just have one to take the edge off. I could never have just one and never could figure out why. I was cursed or blessed that every time I drank more than four drinks, I would have a blackout and forget. Every time I drank, I promised myself that this time I would not have a blackout. It never worked.

While I was home, I went to see my first boyfriend Bill. He was now out of jail. I still can't believe it, but he was not mad that I had not waited and still wanted to be with me. The fact that I wanted to see him solidified that I should not be married. I had no conscience, or guilt. He wanted me to get a divorce and be with him but I did not want to be with him. Years later I would call him and tell him I changed my mind, but he would no longer want me. I wonder why?

I wanted to be free. I wanted excitement, and I did not like the responsibility of being married. I wanted to do whatever I wanted, whenever I wanted, without any boundaries. I had been raised in isolation, and I wanted to live without being responsible for anyone. Now it was legal for me to drink, because I was twenty-one. I did not think about being a parent or what that would entail.

The day I returned home from the wedding was the day of the family pictures. Larry's family was so happy that I was back. If you looked at the pictures you would know what I was thinking. I felt empty inside. Void of feeling.

"I am so glad you are back," Larry said. "I missed you so much."

I could not look at him. My poor husband had no idea what I was planning. He thought I was happy and that we would have a wonderful life together. He did not deserve the pain I would cause. He had done nothing wrong. Between my lack of family skills and the drinking that I had started, he didn't stand a chance.

We were at his mom's house. The entire family was there. After the pictorials were over, I said, "I need to talk to you."
I had only been home less than a day. We hadn't been alone yet.
"Could we go into the other room?"
"Sure," he said, not knowing what was coming. As soon as we got to the room, I closed the door and looked at him in the eye. There was no turning back.
"I want a divorce. I need to be free."
I thought he would have a seizure. He had epilepsy. I had not even considered that. I was too caught up in my own agenda. He looked white. He certainly was not prepared. I felt better telling him with his family there because he could not scream. I turned and walked away.

As soon as we got home from his mom's house, I left, found a job, and got an apartment. One day when I came home from work, he was standing by the stairs, crying.

"Please, don't leave me," he begged. "I'll do whatever you want." I felt nothing.

Sometimes I would come home from work and he would be there to serenade me with his accordion. He was an expert player and had taken lessons from a very famous teacher. No matter what he did, it could not get to my heart.

I couldn't seem to get over the memories of being hit by my mom until I stopped crying, when I was just a toddler. Feeling anything got you hurt. I was void.

I have always regretted leaving him; he was a really nice person. The only thing he did wrong was marry me.

When I hear an accordion playing today, I still think of Larry.

FREE BUT NOTHING TO GIVE

I was certain that this was the thing to do. Thank God for my son. I do not know what would have happened to me, if it had not been for the responsibility of taking care of him. Even with him, I was not capable of being a mom.

There's no other word for it. I was a terrible mother. I didn't hit him but I had nothing to offer him at this time. "You cannot give what you do not have." I had no skills, no family, and no one to give me advice on how to be a mom. I was completely on my own based on my upbringing. I had no idea what to do but I knew I didn't want him to hurt. I did my very best, but it was not very good.

When you see shows on the TV about moms leaving their kids alone, I did that. I only did it once, and it seemed fine at the time. He was sleeping and I couldn't afford a babysitter. I wanted to go out to the bar down the street. I wouldn't be that far away and I wouldn't be gone that long.

I always stayed until last call.

WORKING HARD FOR THE MONEY

I had lots of jobs because I would lose lots of jobs, because of the terrible hangovers.

I was once a proofreader for a calendar company. I also got a job as an undercover worker for a detective agency. My first assignment was to work in a factory to find out why they could not keep white people. The owners thought they were being intimidated. I was there about an hour and I figured it out. These people had to take a bus for two hours to work because it was the only job they could find. They were underpaid, it was filthy, the work was hard, and it didn't have lunch facilities. I had to send a daily report and then the agency would send it to the owner. No one was supposed to know who I was but, I was the only white person there.

The people were really nice. I could not keep up. We only had to cap every third can of hair spray, but with me, it was like a scene from I Love Lucy. They had to get all the ones I missed because it was going way too fast for me. It was good that they thought that was funny.

I also worked in a glue factory and had to cap hot bottles of glue. The bottles burned my hands but I could keep up. It was so hot with the hot glue, and it was not air-conditioned.

The worst and weirdest was working for a sporting goods manufacturer, punching holes in footballs. It paid one cent for every football. I was in serious trouble. The ladies doing it had been there for years and they were fast. I got fired when I asked if the punch press was supposed to have a safety guard.

I really wanted to be a microbiologist and discover the cure for cancer and the common cold, but that no longer seemed possible without an education, money, or family to help with my son.

I didn't think I would ever have a good job; I only went to ninth grade. When I looked for a job, I assumed no one would hire me so I did not try.

I needed to find someone to take care of me.

STUCK ON PILLS

My hangovers were brutal. I went to the doctor and told him I felt like sleeping all of the time. He did not examine me or do tests. He just said I had a thyroid problem and gave me 30mg Dexedrine. I never missed another day of work.

I took my pill in the morning and drank to come down at night. It was the only time the pain went away.

The pain of the abuse of my foster mother, the abandonment of my stepdad, and the abandonment of my real mother would stay with me for most of my life.

I got my pills from a cardiologist. When he told me that he would not prescribe them for me anymore, I told him if he didn't give them to me I would get them off of the street. He continued to give them to me for twelve more years. I could not miss a day or I would become comatose.

DOUBLE TROUBLE?

Larry, my ex-husband, took little Jimmy on weekends. Then I could really party.

I always got in trouble driving. I went up an exit ramp and drove down a sidewalk, but the strangest was when I had a hit and run and the police did not ticket me. They kept my car and asked me where I wanted to go. I told them to take me to the bar by my house. They went with me, stayed, and bought me drinks. They brought my car the next day.

I am the only person I know that got a DUI on my way to court for a DUI. I was so scared about going to court that I went to an all night bar until it was time to go to court. When I got arrested, they told me to leave my car on the road and took me to the station. When I got out, I called a cab and had the driver take me to my car. I showed up for court still drunk, but I got out of both DUI'S. At that time, you just needed money.

CHAPTER 4
A BAD "C" MOVIE

Ryan, I wish most of this was not true but I can assure you that it is, and this is just beginning. Last night, you spent the night so your mom could go to court. Her son, your half brother, moved out to his dad's house because he was smoking pot. Will it ever end? It feels strange writing this while you are sleeping. You look like the angel. I know you are. You are only five. I will pray that God puts a protective shield around you to keep you safe from the nightmare of addiction for eternity.

MADAM GULLIBLE

I don't remember how it came about but I met a girl and asked her to be my roommate. One day she asked if she could use my car while I worked. I was very naïve and trusting so I said, "Sure!" I got a ride home and discovered a completely empty apartment. Not even a piece of silverware was left. Everything was gone. I did not tell the police. I wasn't sure who she was. I believed everything she had told me. I thought we were friends. Now, I didn't even have a bed for my child.

My landlord felt sorry for me and gave me a bed. I found a small bookcase in the garbage. I had two kitchen chairs with no backs and a card table. Someone gave me a couch and a TV.

* * * * * * * * *

I had a guy over to my apartment after a date. I went to check on my son and when I came out of the bedroom, the guy was holding my rent money in his hand. My rent money was hidden in the freezer, so he must have looked for some ice for his drink and found it there.

"What are you doing?" I asked jokingly.

He laughed, "What are you talking about?" waving the money in my face. It was everything I had in the whole world. I was getting scared. I knew I had to fight to get that money back.

"I'll call the police…" I bluffed.

"Prove it," he said, hitting his palm with the stack of cash.

So, I begged "Please, don't take my money. It is all I have."

He left laughing, waving goodbye with the money. There was nothing I could do. I felt weak and unable to help myself.

The following day, I had to think of a way to get some money for my rent. I did not have much time. I called my mom for the first time since I got married. She was the only person I knew that had enough money to help me.

"Mom something terrible has happened," I trembled. "I've been robbed. All of my money was taken. Please help me. I cannot pay my rent. I will be thrown out of my apartment with my son and be put on the street."

She listened silently through my story and without hesitation said, "You made your bed; now live with it," and then hung up. Maybe I should have told her about the furniture being stolen too.

I never asked for her help again.

THE BIG RED DOORS

I liked going to a little neighborhood bar three blocks from my house, so I wouldn't have far to drive. They played good music on the juke box. I knew all the words to the songs. Frank Sinatra and Dean Martin were my favorites and I could sing along. The drinks were all free bought by the regulars or the bartender.

I lived in a town with mostly Italians. One night, a very powerful looking man came into the bar, someone I had never seen before. He was a big man and looked very successful. He was wearing a black shirt, a dark jacket, and a huge diamond ring on his pinky finger. He looked like someone you would not mess with. I liked that. He looked exciting.
"Hi, why haven't I seen you before?" he said.
I smiled, flirting.
"I'm having a party next Saturday. I would like you to come."
It sounded like an order, but I liked his confidence.
"Sure," I said. "Where do you live?"

"The house down the street with the big red doors," he said.

I had driven past that house every day on the way to my apartment. I always wondered who lived in that house. I dressed as nice as I could, black dress, slinky pumps, got a babysitter, and went to his house. I was very excited. I rang the doorbell. The butler answered. I was very impressed. This was my first time being around power and money. In fact, it was my first time going to a party, so I had no idea what to expect.

There were lots of people there and the women were gorgeous. They all looked like models. The men were mostly gruff looking, well dressed, spoke with Italian accents, and wore lots of jewelry. I loved the house. It was professionally decorated with expensive furnishings. I had only seen houses like this in magazines. This man obviously made a lot of money.

I noticed people whispering. People were coming and going. "What's going on?" I asked one of the gorgeous girls.

She must have thought I was part of their group. She said, "They went to the airport to whack someone."

I was definitely with the wrong bunch of people. I wanted to go home. I told them that I needed to go because my babysitter needed to go home. The butler pointed a gun at me and told me that the babysitter had been taken care of and that I wasn't leaving because his boss wanted me to stay. I never found out how they knew where I lived. They had sent a babysitter to my house. After they let me go, I hoped I would never see these people again. I always took a different way home so I never had to go past his house again.

This is just one of many bad decisions on my part. I was still very impressed with power. I knew this man was mob connected. I had heard his name many times. It was exciting and scary at the same time. It would not be my last time getting involved with the syndicate.

A NEW PLAN

The bars that I went to were dark, gloomy, dirty, and loud. I had never been to nice places. I liked going to a bar by my house that was open 24 hours because they never had last call. Pool tables, loud music, and bad, nasty people hung out there. I would go in on Friday and come out on Sunday afternoon.

When I came out, the blaring sun would make me sick but I kept going back. I could do this because of the diet pills I was taking. Sometimes I didn't sleep or eat for days.

There were always really bad fights at the bar, but no one ever stopped them. One night a man was crawling up the stairs and they stomped on his head. His eyes popped out. It didn't faze me. I was oblivious to everything. No feeling, I was completely shut down.

MAYBE THIS TIME

One day after I had been divorced about a year, I went to a different sleazy bar that had a band because I wanted to dance. A man came up to me and said, "Hi, I'm Don. Do you want to dance?"

I didn't recognize him at first but it was the man from the trailer park that I used to drink with. We laughed about running into each other again. I told him I was now divorced and that my roommate had moved out with my furniture. I knew absolutely nothing about him other than he was divorced and that he worked nights and drank days.

I asked him why he was divorced. He told me he had moved out of his house while his wife went to visit her mom in another country. When she came back with nowhere to go, she had to live with his mom and dad. They had two kids, and he told me that he didn't pay child support. I didn't hear any of this.

"Why don't we move in together," Don suggested.
"Only if we get married," I said jokingly.
"Sure!" he said.

We found an apartment, bought all new furniture; and got married. It seemed like the logical thing to do because I kept getting myself in trouble with the wrong kind of people. He seemed nice enough. Feelings never entered into it. The day we got married, we went to an all night bar, and didn't come home until the sun was coming up. I was still clueless, numb, and self-destructive.

MY FAVORITE JOB, BUT NOT FOR LONG

I got a job as a cocktail waitress, which I loved. It was an exclusive bar where mob people hung out. I loved the power and the attention.

The men, mostly Italian, were very nice to me and never hit on me because they knew I had a little boy. To them, family is everything. One day I told them my son was sick and they gave me a $100 bill. I was the only cocktail waitress and was making $150 a night in 1969. It was a lot more money than the glue factory and it was a very exciting environment.

One night someone came in and ordered drinks for the whole place then left without paying. The owner was mad and told me that he had called the police. Then after an hour, the man came back. He called me outside and said, "You called the police!"

"No, it wasn't me," I insisted. He did not believe me. He was furious.

The police had been watching this place. They were looking for a reason to question these people for a variety of reasons but never could bring them in. When they were called for something suspicious, they could bring them in for questioning.

The place emptied out. I had no idea that I should be very afraid.

"You called the police and now I am in trouble with the guys for getting them arrested," he said.

"No, I didn't. I didn't call them, I swear. It was the owner." He took me to the back and threw me into a booth. It was dark. No one else was there. He hit me so hard in the face that my teeth went through my lip. Then, he left. I was sitting in a big restaurant all alone in the dark wondering what to do. I had to drive myself to the hospital. I had six stitches and eight loose teeth.

I couldn't work so I went to the restaurant to collect my check. I pulled in behind the restaurant. A car pulled up in front and another pulled in back of my car. "Leave if you know what's best," the driver said. I couldn't leave fast enough. I was really scared.

They found out where I lived and a big black car would sit in the parking lot as a threat for months. Every time I looked out my window, they were there.

Even today, I get blamed for sending those people to jail. I went into a restaurant not too long ago and the bartender asked me to leave. He said I was the one that caused the trouble forty years ago. They never forget.

MY BLACK AND BLUE WORLD

This time of my life is very dark. I am not proud of it at all. I hope that you never have to go through some of these things that I went through, Ryan, because they leave a permanent mark in the soul.

It must have started with an argument but shortly after we were married, Don beat me. I remember him bringing his hand back and hitting me so hard, he broke my nose. The blood spurted from the floor to the ceiling on the wall. I was more shocked with seeing all of that blood than being hit. My nose was flat to my face. My eyes and face swelled shut. He laughed every time he looked at me because he thought I looked funny. How heartless could he be? He had no remorse.

My mom hit me, but never like this. No one deserves to be hit. I didn't understand. I had no defense against a man hitting me. I couldn't fight back to defend myself, but then again, no one should have to. My son was only two. He saw what happened to his mom. I could not explain it to him because I didn't understand it myself. At that time, they didn't have shelters and I'm not sure I would have gone. Since I came from violence, I was used to abuse.

I was now in a very bad situation with nowhere to go and no one to ask for help. I knew some very powerful people that would come to my defense. I was friends with a hit man who lived directly across the street from us. He was Italian. I was like a daughter to him, and, to him, family was everything. They never hit their wives. He knew us very well. We had part of our wedding reception at his bar. My husband would be in serious trouble if he found out what happened to my face. He could arrange for my husband to be killed, but I was not going to tell anyone.

I stayed in isolation until I healed. Don promised to never do it again. I believed him.

We moved to another house where I got pregnant. I was excited about having another baby. Don's friend was living with us. I didn't need more work and I resented his friend living with us for nothing. I asked Don to have him leave and he got angry. He pushed me and hit me over and over again. I fell on a heater. I had a swollen face and a black eye. I was six months pregnant and I was sure I would lose the baby, but I didn't. He felt no remorse and said I deserved it for telling him what to do.

We had only been married for about a year. I felt so alone. I had no one to turn to. I was helpless and in the midst of a mess. Why did this keep happening?

I had a son and another on the way. I was sure it would get better. I was only twenty-four and had no idea what to do with my life. I always thought I had made the right decision and was always surprised when it didn't work out.

* * * * * * * * * *

God blessed me with nausea and I never wanted to drink with either child. Thank you God, because at that time we did not know the danger of drinking while pregnant.

When my son Scott, your dad, was born, the delivery was tedious and took seventeen hours of intense labor, the same as with Jim. I took no drugs at all. I had a very high pain tolerance. I attributed that to all of my beatings. But seeing little Scott for the first time was worth all the pain. I felt like I had a renewed purpose for living. He was a beautiful baby. He always had a sense of wonder in his eyes. He was a great baby from the start and slept through the night the first month.

Scott was a beautiful child with fine features and beautiful dark eyes that could look into your soul. He had a huge amount of straight black hair that was as soft as down. One day when I went in to feed him, the black hair had fallen out completely overnight and was replaced with blonde fluff. But it didn't matter; blonde or black, I loved his hair and I loved him just the same. I loved having children and still wanted six children.

Scott gave my life meaning. I was willing to endure the pains for him and for Jim, even though I still had no direction in my life. I continued to harbor the unhealthiness that I carried in my childhood.

I got another job as a cocktail waitress. I never saw my husband. I would leave when he got home, and then I would go out after work. I worked in a very nice steakhouse where politicians and lawyers hung out. More money, more power. Just being in that environment felt good. And it was also good to be physically away from Don, where I wouldn't run the risk of being his punching bag.

A BAD TWENTY-FOUR HOURS

We lived on an alley. Our house was on one end and the tavern was on the opposite end. One night I heard a big explosion. A man driving down the alley ran into the back of our house. When I opened the door, the dog got out and got hit by a car. My husband didn't know it, but I was seeing a counselor for the abuse and the appointment was thirty miles away. I had to travel because it was free. When I went out to get into my car, it was gone, stolen with all of the Christmas presents that I had stored in the trunk so no one would know. Being desperate, I decided to take the bus. I had to transfer twice. It was freezing rain. I was so cold. I stood at the bus stop wondering if I could endure the commute when a nice car pulled up with two well dressed men.

"Do you want a ride?" the guy said. He seemed nice.

"Yes!" as I got into the back seat, grateful to be out of the cold and freezing rain. As soon as I got into the car, the man flashed a badge and said I was being charged with prostitution.

"WHAT?!" I burst into tears and explained the last twenty-four hours and my reason for going to counseling. They felt sorry for me and not only took me to the appointment, but waited and gave me a ride home. The whole day was like a bad C movie that ended in a good note.

Ryan, I knew the first husband twenty-nine days and the second one, other than the drinking time at the trailer park, a couple of months. I was looking for someone to take me away from the abuse at my mom's house but gravitated into a violent situation. I was helpless to help myself and got myself into a bigger mess. It is so sad that abuse repeats itself, based on the past. No one deserves emotional or physical abuse. Do not EVER hit a woman; she has no defense. If you get that angry, leave and stay gone until you can resolve your own issues. If you argue, fight fair. Remember words are like bullets; they wound your heart and can never be taken back. I heard of a couple that hold hands and say a prayer every night for each other before they go to bed. What a great idea. Even if you are angry it would make it all better. Ryan, when you get married, do this for me

CHAPTER 5
A TURNING POINT

HELPLESS, BATTERED AND ALONE

One beautiful Sunday afternoon, Don started an argument again. He had been drinking. I remember him telling me to shut up. I guess I didn't because he jumped up and hit me in the face. My lips and nose were bleeding. "Please stop," as I ran to the bedroom and shut the door. I had never called the police because I was afraid what he would do if they arrested him and he got out. This time I had to get him away from me. I ran to the bedroom and slammed the door. Then I called the police. I was sure they would arrest him for domestic violence.

I was so scared; he was trying to break down the door. I prayed the police would get there quickly and take him away.

When they came, I explained what happened. "Take him away," I said. They told me to stay in my room, while they talked to him. They came back and told me he agreed not to hit me again and then left. I thought, "Please don't leave me!!"

As soon as they left, he beat me again. There was nowhere to go. I was completely helpless, battered, and alone.

* * * * * * * * *

I made a decision to die; there was no other escape. I could not take any more abuse. Dying would end it. I didn't think I had any other choice. I felt my children would be better off. There was no one that would miss me. I felt completely useless. I was not capable of making any good decisions.

I took pills and cough medicine. When Don got home, he found me lying on the bathroom floor and took me to the hospital. I got my stomach pumped and was in intensive care for the first time. I told myself, "Next time I will need to take more."

At that time, if you tried to commit suicide you were released to psychiatric care. I was anxious to get started with treatment. I needed a lot of help with the depression and helplessness of my life.

When I went to the psychiatrist office, I was relieved I would get help and finally have someone to confide in. He instructed me to lie down on the couch. I began telling him about my life. All of a sudden he lay down next to me, telling me how much he liked me. I jumped up. I was at my lowest mentally; I got sick to my stomach. I couldn't even trust the doctors to help me. I couldn't trust anyone. I felt more helpless than before.

What was happening to my life? I couldn't kill myself, and I couldn't get professional help. I was living in hell, with nowhere to go and no way out.

We were just getting ready to move into a condo that had been built. A brand new place to live and two new cars seemed enough to make me stay for security's sake, but it wasn't. We had been married for two of the longest years in my life.

STRENGTH I DIDN'T KNOW I HAD

Misery has a way of bringing out the best survival instincts. I remember looking out the window one day, a short time later, and thinking about what I should do. I decided, "I cannot live like this anymore." I had no idea how I would make it work. For the first time, I didn't have a plan. There were no tears, was no fear. I looked at my children's faces and saw the pain and the fear that they were experiencing living in the abuse. It was affecting them as much as me. I had to find a way to take care of them and me. I had nowhere to go, no family, no job, no education, no money, and two little children, one and five.

But it was clear to me that I could not let someone abuse me anymore. I didn't know where to look for an apartment, what town to live in, or if I would find a job. I left with the clothes on my back. I knew that wherever I went, I would still be better off than where I was at that point. So, it didn't matter where I was going; I just had to go. I walked out with my kids and never looked back.

TAKING CONTROL OF MY LIFE

God was always with me, guiding my every move. I had no idea where to go and get help but the next thing you know I was guided to the township office. They gave me $500. I then went to the county and they gave me a government subsidy for an apartment and child care. I found an ad in the paper for a dental receptionist.

I showed up with kids in tow.

"If you hire me and give me a chance, I will work for nothing, until I learn," I said to the dentist, looking him straight in the eye.

He must have seen my determination, which was fueled by survival. He hired me and I became his office manager for the next fourteen years.

I went from there to get an apartment. I found a really nice apartment in a new town, hoping to have a new start. It was great; it had two bedrooms and two baths. The only problem was it was a ghetto area. Gangs lived there. You just had to get through the parking lot and then it was nice. I would live in that area for fourteen years. I did all of this the first day that I left my husband.

The next day I went to a furniture store and bought everything for my new apartment. I remember the payments were eleven dollars a month. I still have some of the same furniture and that was thirty-nine years ago.

I have often thought that determination is the key to success, not motivation. If you are determined, you can do anything. My motto is "I can do this."

I never give up.

TOO MUCH RESPONSIBILITY

Don did not want to pay child support and said he did not have enough money for the divorce. It would take me four years to save the money for the divorce and he only paid child support occasionally. At that time no one knew, and I did not fight.

Every time Don saw me, he would tell me that I would never be able to take care of myself. My mother always told me that also. This is very common for abusive people to say because they want you to turn your life over to them, so they can control it.

The only problem was I did not make enough money to support my family. I had to get a second job as a cocktail waitress working three nights a week.

The only way I could do it was amphetamine pills. I got off at two in the morning from the bar and had to be back at work, at the dentist office by eight. I would have to have a couple of drinks to get to sleep for this short time. My son Jim had to wake me every morning to get me to work on time. If it was difficult to wake me, he would be in trouble. There was a movie called All That Jazz. In it, the main character would get up every day, pop a pill, and put eye drops in his bloodshot eyes to get into the day. Then, he would drink to come down at night. This was how I lived for seven years. After Jim got me up, he had to get his brother and himself to school. This has haunted me all of my life. I denied my son a childhood. He had to be responsible for me, and his brother.

YOU NEED TO KNOW

Ryan, I am sure all of this is too difficult to process. I am sorry if this information is hurting you. I would never do anything to intentionally hurt you. I am telling you all of this for two reasons: One, it has never been told. Two, you will be able to see what addiction does to your family's lives and hopefully it will make a difference.

Your dad, your uncle Jim, two cousins, my mom, my grandmother, your grandfather, on my side, and I are all alcoholics. The list goes on and on.

The difference for you is, you are the only one with a dad, and he is a wonderful dad. He has set an example for you. Follow his lead.

Don't pretend that you will be OK. It is in your genes; even if you are raised in a sober home the chances are, you are still predisposed.

Don't pick up the first drink.

You will see the horrible consequences of alcoholism in my life. You know the ending but it sure was hard getting there. Enter into these difficult spaces in my memory so that you can be warned of how bad it gets when you lose control of your life because of addiction. If you think right now that what you have read so far is terribly bad, be worried that it is going to get a lot worse. I have not yet reached my bottom.

CHAPTER 6
MONEY AND POWER

BROKEN HEARTED ME

Because I was the cocktail waitress in a very nice steakhouse as a supplement to my dental office job, I met many successful people every day drinking in the bar. It never occurred to me that normal people don't go to bars every day to drink. But then, I was not normal. I didn't even know what normal was.

One particular man got my attention. He was short, heavy, 52, (I was 27), and very successful. He was so funny. I don't remember ever really laughing until I met him. His name was Tom.

Tom felt sorry for me and I was really naïve about his motivation. He was married with seven kids so I asked myself "what would he want with me?"

He started taking me to really nice places and buying me expensive clothes. Four hundred dollar dresses, forty years ago. That was how much my rent was! I didn't know that I should not let him do that. I loved the prestige, the attention. He bought a car that was my favorite color and then bought me a very expensive dress to match. I had never had any of this before. I was very impressed. He even took me to business events.

He told me how unhappy he was at home. I thought I could help him get through a bad marriage because he made me feel so special. I was starting to have strong feelings for him because of everything he was doing for me. I can honestly say, even though the relationship was crazy, he taught me how to feel loved, for the first time, or what I thought was love.

He was very kind to my children, buying them clothes and giving me money for them. We even took them on a trip.

One day while I was at work, he painted my apartment. No one had ever done anything for me like that. I did not know how to feel or think.

Tom drank a lot. Everything centered on drinking. I would wait for him to come over and he would call and say he was on his way, but some of the time, he wouldn't make it and he always promised not to do it again. Each time I believed him.

He was married, but now I was determined to get him to leave his wife. I had no concern for the seven kids. They never entered my mind. I needed him for me!

We had been together two years. Compared to the past, they had been the best so far. On Christmas, he gave me a mink coat. Two days later on my birthday, he proposed to me and gave me the most elaborate diamond ring I have ever seen. It was really expensive. I know because I had to get it insured the next day. He was going to give me the money to finalize my divorce. He had filed for divorce and I was finally going to have someone to take care of me. I had been waiting for someone like him to give my life a new beginning, and to take care of me the rest of my life.

A very short time later, he suddenly became unavailable. "Did he have a heart attack and no one knew to call me?" I was scared. He would not answer his phone. I went to the bars to find him. What had happened to my fiancée? I had a ring on my finger, which cost as much as a house, but my man was nowhere to be found. Where was my knight that would rescue me and provide for me and my family?

I went to his apartment. He had a key to mine but I did not to his. I stood there in front of his door. I could hear voices. I did not know who they were. I just wanted someone to tell me where my fiancé was. I rang the bell, without second thoughts.

A female answered the door. I would not call her a lady, was my first impression. Who was she? I did not know what she was doing in my man's apartment. "Maybe she's the cleaning lady," I thought.

"Is Tom home?" I asked.

"Who are you?" she replied indifferently.

"Who are YOU?" I said. I felt she needed to explain to me first, since I was the one with the ring on my finger.

"I'm Tom's girlfriend!" she said, as if I should know.

I felt like someone had punched me in the stomach. Where did she come from? Wasn't he spending all of his time with me?

"What's going on here?" I demanded, almost screaming.

Tom came to the door.

"Who is THAT person," I screamed, "and what is she doing here?"

"After I gave you the ring, I was afraid of our age difference and found someone else. I am going to marry her," Tom said, without any expression or feeling.

I was devastated. Without thinking, I took off the ring and threw it at him. I should have kept it. BIG MISTAKE!

Tom did marry her, but died of cirrhosis of the liver a few years later, caused by his alcoholism.

NOT KNOWING HOW TO LIVE

This was the first time I had let anyone see a little of my heart. He broke it and stomped on it. The pain was unbearable.

I thought about it for what seemed like an eternity. I felt that God had abandoned me and a self-inflicted death was worth the price of burning in hell forever. It seemed better than the hell I was in. This time I would take enough pills that no one could survive. Working for the dentist, I ordered 100 pain pills and 100 diet pills that were half pain pill and half diet pill. I swallowed them with beer. Instantly, everything became a blur. I fell to the floor; I do not know who called the ambulance.

The doctor said that it was a miracle. He told me that I had taken enough pills to kill an elephant and should not have even made it to the ambulance.

For many years, I did not recognize how significant that miracle was. God had a mission for me and he was not going to allow me to interfere with the plan. Yesterday at church, I was reliving this very event and thinking about God's mercy. I imagined what God was saying: "No child, it is not time. I have a plan for you."

When I regained consciousness, my hands and feet were strapped with leather straps to the bed. I do not know how long I was unconscious but when I came to, I was so surprised. Who was standing there, but Don my husband that I had been separated from for two years, and Tom, the man that had just broken my heart. I hated both of them. I do not know what they were doing there or how they knew what happened. I asked them both to leave.

I was completely unable to move. I had no choice but to stare at the ceiling and think about why I survived. The bed was covered in blood from me being sick after they pumped my stomach. My throat felt like it had a sponge in it, no moisture whatsoever. I could not swallow, it was so dry. When the nurse came in, I said," Could I please have a drink of water?"

She looked at me with complete distain and said the most powerful statement that would change my life forever:

"No! If you want to die, die… I am here to help people that want to live."

She walked out, leaving me with the parched throat. I was so angry that she would not give me a drink of water. I worked all day at removing the restraints so when she came back I could kick her in the chest when she came near me. She never came back and I never got a drink of water.

I suddenly realized that I didn't want to die; I just didn't know HOW TO LIVE!

Many people try to kill themselves for attention. I can assure you I wanted to die every day. I would cross the days off the calendar as if I were in prison. Every day was one less day I had to live. I hated my life and couldn't even die right.

My mom and my husband were right. I was a loser and would never be able to take care of myself. I was only twenty-seven. How much longer did I have to live? Nothing I did worked out. There was no one to talk to. I was all alone.

I felt like God was punishing me for everything I had ever done. My soul was sick. I would never pray again, I thought. I did not know until many years later, that you can choose how you feel. Happiness is an inside job. You cannot have an emotion without thinking it first. People choose to be miserable, but I could not stop it at that time. Since then, I have learned how to be happy. It was a process. *I survived, in spite of myself, to be able to tell you this story, Ryan. Thank you God!*

CHAPTER 7
THEY LIKE ME, THEY REALLY LIKE ME

NEED TO BE LOVED

I had no problem finding a man and was never without a man in my life, for even a day. Men thought I was fun. I liked racing cars and riding motorcycles. I loved the danger. I even took a motorcycle driving course. I would do everything from whitewater rafting to fishing and camping, and I really had fun. I was their kind of girl.

I always made sure my relationships overlapped. When I was ready to discard someone, I made sure there was someone else waiting. No one would ever get to my heart and hurt me again. I had completely shut down.

My relationships usually lasted a year and were not just casual dating. It was calculated and cunning. I needed help and someone to take care of me.

My epitaph would be "I Did It My Way." I used men to fulfill my needs, and they were very accommodating. I was heartless, unfeeling, and uncaring. I did whatever I had to do to survive.

MY ADDICTION

My addiction to alcohol was terrible. If I did something that bothered me, I would drink to cover it up. I really never processed anything or worked it out. The pain of my foster mom beating me and the pain that my real mom didn't want me was there every time I drank. It was a knot in my stomach that would only go away unless I was anesthetized.

Even sober, I had no conscience. My life was consumed with self. It is a disease of self-centeredness and selfish behavior. Everything was always someone else's fault. It was always my way or not at all.

I went on a date once and brought my drink. He told me to throw out the drink or I had to get out. I told him to let me out. He didn't.

The kids thought my behavior was normal, because they had never been around anything else. They wanted to install a refrigerator in the car for my beer because I always took my beer with us.

I had no family to confront me, no time for friends, and I did not like women. The only relationship I ever had with a woman was my mother. I did not trust any women.

I practiced controlled drinking. I would only have a couple when I went out and would drink more when I got home. I would only drink beer. It made perfect sense to me. If I only had one bottle an hour, it was OK. Most of the time, I drank at home because it was safe.

I only got drunk a couple of times a year, but I could never tell when that was going to be or what I would do when it happened. I almost ran my car into someone's house because he made me angry. Men were afraid of what I would do if angered. I was afraid too, because now I had thoughts of killing them with a knife and I didn't know what I would do when I was drinking. I was out of control.

One day I went to a bar that I liked. Everyone turned their heads, when I walked in and would not talk to me. I asked why? They said, "We don't want to talk about it." I never found out what I did. It was a good thing that I had blackouts because I could not remember most of my drinking. No one ever suspected that I had too much to drink when I was out. I could talk without slurring but when I stood up to walk, I would fall to the floor. I tried not to stand up but since I drank beer, it didn't take long.

I was always losing my car. I would have someone drive me home, but I could never remember where the car was. When I woke up in the morning I would run to the window to see if my car was there. Sometimes it wouldn't be there and I would have to try and retrace where I had been. These were some of my scariest times of my life.

THE ILLUSION

Everything seemed fine, but I had nothing to compare to.

My son's best friend was always at my house. His mom was having an affair, so she asked me if I would go out with her husband to get him out of the house. Seemed like a plan. He was nice, attractive, and had money. Why not?

I told him I wanted to take my kids to Disney. He said he would pay for it, if I took his son too. Of course I would. We flew down and after one day, his son annoyed me so I sent him home on the next flight. We stayed for a week at his dad's expense.

There was a married man that I met at the bar. He really liked me and must have felt sorry for me. All he ever wanted was to have dinner with me. It was all very innocent. When he took me home he would give me three $100 bills for going out with him. I would insist on not taking the money (I didn't mean it) and he would tell me that if I didn't take it he would send me enough flowers to fill the house. I took it.

For years, I went to counseling to help me with decisions and help raise my kids. Never once did it enter my mind to mention my drinking. I had no idea that my drinking was any different than anyone else. Counselors can only work with what you tell them.

CHAPTER 8
I TRIED TO BE A GOOD MOM

NO ONE TO CORRECT MY MISTAKES

With nothing to go on, I tried to be everything my mom wasn't. I never missed a sporting event, a play, a PTA meeting, anything. I was there.

I really tried. I would take my income tax return every year and take my boys white water rafting in the Smokey's. It was a twelve hour drive and I could do it for $500.

I would get donuts for breakfast and make sandwiches to take for lunch. I even found a good restaurant that served family meals for dinner for three dollars a person.

I tried to do manly things, because they did not have a dad.

I always told them nice things about their dad. I never told them that he didn't send support. One time, to get out of paying, he actually moved to another state. Their dad never came to see them so the only person they had to guide them was me.

The kids sold candy every year to be able to go to camp for two weeks. It was the only time I did not have all the responsibility.

My son would put on torn jeans and stand out in front of the grocery store in February. He always sold enough to pay for camp.

Ryan, your dad was special too, just like you. He would bring me bird feathers, rocks, and he always brought me the first flower of spring, even if it was a dandelion.

I was very serious about discipline. I had to be; there was no one to help.

I always insisted that the boys keep their room clean.

One day, I told them I would be cleaning their room in two days. I told them everything needed to be put away: clothes, game pieces, etc. Everything needed to be put where it was supposed to be or I would throw it out. I always followed through on my threats. I will never forget their surprise when I actually threw out shoes, jackets, toys, and everything that was not put away. I never replaced any of it. After that, they always kept their room clean.

My son still made his bed at twenty-eight. I have never understood why someone would put up with the mess that kids do. It was my house and until they were on their own, they needed to take care of our stuff.

I also had another rule. It was, "keep up or get lost." I was tired of trying to keep track of everyone. I would just walk and they had to keep track of me. What they didn't know was I always knew where they were.

It was a great tool on school field trips. The kids were so scared they would get lost that they kept up. Other moms were always trying to find the slow kids.

I tried to hide my addiction from my kids. I would only drink casually until they were in bed or not at home. I wanted them to think I was a good mom but I had lost my choice not to drink. It was the only time I didn't have sadness and pain. I didn't want to feel anything.

Jim has never forgiven me for taking his childhood away, by making him man of the house. I have apologized many, many, times. His real dad would never see him because he thought I had an affair. It was not true. My son's stepdad was never around. My son had no dad, only a very sick mom, and he was fourteen when I got sober.

I look back to that woman now and try to tell her, "You did the best you knew how." She tells me, "It was not enough." Should I live in regret? Remember Ryan, sometimes there is no going back. Life is going to press. We do not get to proofread it first. Sometimes we do not get second chances.

PARENTING 101

Ryan, here are some things I have learned over the years, which will help you with your family, so hopefully, you will be able to break the cycle of destruction that has plagued our family.

Kids need rules and structure. Kids do not want their parents to be their friend. They need guidance. Every time you came to my house, you knew I meant what I said and could not be manipulated. You had a bedtime and a mealtime. Explain the rules so they understand. A lot of parents just say "do it" or "because I'm your parent." I always explained and you always did what I said because you understood.

Teach your kids about God.

Take your family to church every week.

Teach them about money, how to save and how to spend.

Do not give them more than a couple of gifts. They don't need things; they need you to play with them. The chores will always be there; they will grow up too soon. Value the time you spend with them.

Teach them about charity and helping others so they will understand about giving and sharing. Take them to see the poor and to food banks so they understand about poverty. Remember when I took you to see the family that had the mom, dad, and kids that all slept in the same bed. You finally understood how lucky you were.

Discipline your kids; it's OK if they get mad about it. When you explain do not back down. Be firm. Mean what you say.

Always say "Sorry," when you hurt their feelings.

Don't be afraid of too much affection.

Tuck you kids in at night and pray with them.

Have a bedtime for school nights. Kids need twelve hours of sleep to grow.

Make sure they do well in school. This is their responsibly and will determine their destiny.

Get them involved in team sports; they need to learn how to lose. Life is not about winning, but learning how to lose and to keep trying.

Laugh and be silly. Remember when we would just blow up balloons and let them fly around the room or when we sprayed each other with the hose. It's OK to get wet and dirty.

Ryan, each child has a gift; understand it and nurture it so they will grow with confidence. Make them feel good about themselves. You can never give too much encouragement. Complement them and thank them for helping every chance you get. It does not have to be perfect. It doesn't matter if it is not the way you would do it.

I had a rule about staying home from school. They had to throw up or have a temperature. Everything else required school. They will not be able to stay home from work because they don't feel good enough to go.

When they are teenagers, ALWAYS know the other parents and talk to them before your kids go to their house. Meet the parents; see how they live. Do not just call your kids at their friend's house or let them call you.

God says love everyone and forgive. Teach them how to resolve conflict by example with your wife and neighbors. Kids can be mean, but you can teach them how to deal with it.

Mealtimes are the most important. Make sure you have dinner with your family and talk about their day. This is the most important time of the day.

Don't ever be too busy to listen to how they are feeling.

"A deal is a deal." Always keep your word and make sure they keep theirs to you and others, even if they made a bad deal.

Always let them suffer the consequences of bad behavior. Bad decisions have consequences. Do not defend them. It is better you teach them, than life.

Always make them try different foods and make them eat their meals. It's for their own good, no dessert unless they finish.

Ryan, I hope these suggestions will help you have healthy, happy children. I wish I would have had them.

CHAPTER 9
A RECORD HIGH

UNABLE TO SEE THE SOLUTION

I knew I was looking for something in my life. I knew I had some feeling that something must be better than the life I was leading. But what it was, I did not know. All I had in my mind were bad memories and a lot of ignorance about the world, about the truth and about the things that really matter. Looking around in ignorance can lead you to really dark places. I wish I had not gotten into the dark, but I am also glad that it is through the dark that I saw the light. I heard Father Mike use a fancy word to talk about this – the apophatic way. I learned about the good by seeing what is not good. It's a difficult way. I had to learn in reverse of what others do, because I had no one to teach me, right from wrong.

The diet pills were working great, but I had a hard time coming down at night. I had never smoked marijuana. One night, someone introduced me to what I thought was a miracle drug; I didn't have to feel at all. Marijuana takes away ALL motivation and feeling.

I do not remember how I acquired it but I had nine bricks of pot hidden under my bed. Yes, the real size of a brick. That would probably be enough for an entire city. I never did anything in a small way. If a little was good, a lot was better. Once I was prescribed pain pills for my wisdom teeth, it said to take 2 pills every 4 hours. I took 4 every 2 hours.

You're probably thinking where did I get the money to buy my drugs? I never bought any drugs; someone always gave them to me. No one likes to get high by themselves and they knew I didn't have money. I never paid for drinks out and every time someone came over they brought me drinks too. So basically everyone else was supporting my habit.

THE REAL WARFARE

This was a very dark time in my life. I would put the kids to bed; drink my beer, and smoke pot. And as if that was not really enough, I sought other forms of escape from my personal void.

It was at this time I decided to investigate witchcraft. I felt I should look into Satan. It seemed right since I thought God had abandoned me. I bought a book and decided to do some of the spells, just to see if they would work. I started with simple spells. They had one where you cut a lemon and said some words. I did the Ouija board. It seemed to work too.

I felt I was searching for answers to my terrible life. My soul was sick.

I also started reading the Bible during these times and felt a real warfare going on. One night, I asked God to show me hell. I remember clearly what I saw. I saw a deep pit with people screaming and reaching up, fire all around. If it was an illusion, it was real to me, and I will never forget. I knew I didn't want to be there but I did not know how to stop the downward spiral.

SATAN WAS VERY CLOSE

One day, I was riding the elevator with my new neighbor that had just moved in the next door to me. The pupils of his eyes looked black. He was the most evil person I had ever seen. He made me feel like my skin was crawling and I started shaking.

I don't know why, but I asked him if he was evil. He looked me right in the eye with those dark piercing eyes and said, "Yes." I felt like I had gone to the other side, somewhere powerful and awful. There was no going back. What had I done? What was happening to me? Then he walked straight ahead without looking back into his apartment that was next to mine.

Soon after that, I decided to try and reach the spirit of Houdini. I was really good at meditating. I would go into a trance and focus all of my mind and energy in one direction. I had taken a yoga class on how to do this when I was younger.

I read a description of how to go into a trance. I had headphones on for white noise and my eyes were covered with ping pong balls, cut in half taped on, so I could see a candle flicker through them. This helped me focus. My kids were sitting on the couch watching TV, while I was sitting at the dining table. I was totally focused. All of a sudden, my chair was pulled from the table, about four feet, next to the wall of my neighbor. The headphones flew off of my head. I felt my soul was being pulled from my body and I only had seconds to decide which way to go. The thoughts were real! I could decide to go with Satan and have everything on this earth I ever wanted, but would have to pay the price of hell. Or, I could choose the way that seemed harder. I remembered seeing the people in the pit reaching up and screaming to get out of hell, to no avail. Nothing was worth that.

I felt myself pulling away from the wall. I could not let him take my soul. I was willing to try and live differently. I would give up all of the satanic worship that I had been doing, even if it was on a small scale. I was definitely in dangerous territory.

It all happened so fast and you probably think that I must have been high on alcohol or drugs, but I remember as if it were yesterday. I had a split second to decide. It was thirty-two years ago and I still remember the feelings and the experience.

I never asked my kids what they thought about what had just happened. They were probably used to unusual behavior.

The very next day, I went in search of an exorcist. I was in danger. I felt possessed. I called an Episcopal church and explained what had happened. They did not laugh like I thought they would. They sent me to a Pentecostal church. I called them and they said to come right away.

There were four people there and part of it was like the movie. They placed their hands on my body and said prayers. They asked Satan to leave my body. If I wasn't there, I would not have believed it, but after about an hour, I felt something powerful had happened, I felt Satan was gone. It was a life changing moment. But when would I find God?

I went home and got rid of everything in my house that might be evil, including the books and the Ouija board. I took the pentagon's off the windows and decided I had to move away from the neighbor. I needed another plan. I was scared.

AN ANGEL'S DARE

I needed the evil to be replaced by good, but I did not know where to begin. I found a religious retreat. The title was something like," Do You Want to Feel Better?" I know now I was divinely guided to this place to meet my angel. I had never been to this place before or even knew it existed. It was a beautiful Catholic Retreat House surrounded by water and trees, one of the most peaceful places I had ever been. It was April 1977.

We went to workshops and had great food. I used my free time to just walk around the beautiful grounds.

It lasted for three days. On the last day, I really didn't want to leave. Suddenly, a man showed up that I hadn't seen at the retreat.

"Hi," he said. "Can I walk with you?"
"Sure, why not?"
"Why are you here?" he asked.

The gates opened and I started telling him my whole life, from the abuse and the responsibility of taking care of the kids to my latest evil experience. I left nothing out. I just needed someone to talk to and I didn't care if he was a stranger.

"Do you drink?" he asked.
"Well, not really. I only drink a six-pack a night."
"I think you are an alcoholic." He said, as if he was asking someone for ice cream, just matter of fact.

Who was this man? Who did he think he was? He seemed gentle and sincere, but you can't say those things to strangers. I was offended!

"I don't drink that much. I only get drunk a couple of times a year." To me, drunk was out of control so the six-pack seemed normal to me. It didn't seem like that much.

"There's a way to prove it to yourself," he whispered. You set a limit for thirty days, but you can't save over from the day before or take from the next day. It has to be reasonable. You have to be honest with yourself. If you go over, even once, you are an alcoholic."

No problem!! I could do this. No one would ever have to know. I would prove it to him. I did not have a problem. I only drank my six-pack a day. One an hour from six to midnight wasn't too much. I'll show him!!

I used to buy my six-packs daily on the way home from work. One day, after nine days (but who was counting), the liquor store had a twelve pack for sale. I drank nine. I couldn't control it. The desire was there but once I started I did not want to quit. I would drink what I had. I could never leave wine in the bottle either. He was right. I could not do it. I had a drinking problem, but what would I do about it? I would have to be more careful and really try to control it better.

I believe he was an angel sent by God to bring this to my attention, because everyone else that I associated with was just like me. I never saw or heard from this man again.

ANOTHER PLAN

I had to move away from my neighbor, but I did not know how I would do that.

The man that lived directly downstairs from me was flirting. One day I was sitting on my balcony, and he was on his. He yelled up, "I saw you sitting out. How about we get together sometime?"

I pretended I didn't hear him. He didn't seem my kind of guy, kind of rough. He was charming but not that great looking. One day, he showed up with a big bunch of long-stemmed red roses and a very expensive bottle of wine.

"Hi, my name is Tim. Can I come in?" I could not say no; wine and roses were the way to my heart. I will never forget the look on his face when I pulled out a big glass and filled it with ice for the wine. I liked it that way.

His kids lived with him, and my kids seemed to like them. Sure, he had girls and I had boys. It was very convenient with him living downstairs. I drank his alcohol and smoked his pot. That way, I didn't have to go out. At least I had enough sense not to drive anymore when I drank. That was the only good decision I was capable of making.

We continued the partying for another couple of months. Apparently the trip one floor up the elevator was too much effort because one day he said, "Why don't we get a house together?"

It seemed like a plan to me because then I would have access to his drugs and alcohol plus, my share of the rent would cost less than my apartment. It was a way out. I no longer had to live next to my evil neighbor. I would have someone to share expenses. My lease was up in August. It had been four months since my retreat and I had forgotten everything about being an alcoholic.

We got the house. There were more drugs than I ever thought possible. I did not know at that time that he was also a drug dealer. I did it again? He is another man with issues?! When I got myself into trouble, I was always surprised.

It was a nuthouse. He had two girls, I had two boys, and I found out recently that the kids were actually smoking pot when I wasn't home. People kept coming and going. I had no idea Tim was selling drugs. I convinced my coworkers and even the dentist to smoke pot. We were having parties at the dentist's house. I smoked pot at the dentist's office on the days that he didn't come in. When the phone rang, I just looked at it and let it ring.

When I wasn't high or drinking I was convinced that I was losing my mind. I was completely out of control, unable to function. I went back to counseling; I obviously had some serious problems. I was crazy. I never told the counselor about the alcohol or drugs because I didn't think it was a problem.

IT SEEMED LIKE THE ONLY WAY OUT

I spent a lot of time thinking about my life and what the problem could be. I started drinking at fifteen, seriously at twenty-one. I had been taking pills since I was twenty-one and had been smoking pot for the last year. Even sober, I was crazy. I had never dealt with any problems. I had always escaped reality and didn't have any reality left in my life anymore. Plus, I had no coping skills.

It must have been sheer desperation that made me decide that my children were the problem. I had tried everything possible to turn my life around and I kept going in circles. I thought, if I didn't have my children, I would be free. I thought I had too much responsibility. I had nowhere to send them, no family to help. I had no idea where their father was. I couldn't do it all alone anymore. Then, I came up with the ultimate solution: *I would kill them and bury them in the backyard.* I thought about this for a month, sober. I had a plan. I told no one.

On the day that I set out to do this, I left work at noon and went to bars. I needed to drink to do this. Remember how I always had a blackout after four drinks? Not on this day! I drank everything from Bacardi's to Manhattans, champagne, and beer, but nothing was happening. I was drinking all day but could not get drunk. I remember everything that happened that day.

I could not send the children to their dad, I could not kill myself, and now I am living with a drug dealer. I could no longer handle any reality. I seemed to have no other option.

I headed home after drinking all day, still feeling sober, which was making me angry. I kept repeating the reasons in my head. This would be the answer. Eliminate the children. I would no longer have all of that responsibility. I would be free. I would like to say that I feared for their lives and thought that it was a bad decision, but I didn't think about their safety at all. I was only thinking about what would happen to me if I got caught.

I was sitting in my living room, contemplating what I wanted to do. I felt trapped. I wanted them gone forever, but I did not want to go to jail. I was very frustrated that I could not do anything about my problems. I got angrier than I had ever been. I started breaking everything from the glass tables and the lamp to the fish tank. I remember watching the fish flopping on the floor.

I was completely out of control. The rage was taking over. A counselor told me once that rage is the opposite of terror. I had lived with terror almost all of my life. Now, all of my rage was surfacing and I was fuming.

My older son called the police. I said to myself, now he really would die, how dare him. Just wait until the police leave. When the police arrived, I was standing in the middle of total destruction.

They came bursting into the house. They asked Tim what had happened.

"She just went nuts, breaking everything in sight," Tim said.

"We're going to have to arrest her for disorderly conduct. Are you willing to sign a complaint?," they asked Tim.
"Sure." He said.

Great! Now I have a drug dealer having me arrested. Why didn't I report him? I think I was just scared about what they were going to do with me.

"You can't arrest me!" I said emphatically.
"I'm a lady and I live in a nice town. How dare you threaten to arrest me…"
I told them this as they handcuffed me and threw me into the police car. The handcuffs were really tight. They were hurting my wrist.
"Please loosen them," I requested.

They ignored me. I had never been arrested before. They booked me on disorderly conduct. I was really scared.

The bail was $25. I had $22. If you ever need someone to bring you $3 to get out of jail, ask for $300. No one wanted to get out of bed at 2 am to bring me the money. I could hear the metal doors clanking; I was going to be in one of those cells if I didn't get $3.

They were willing to let me call until I came up with the money. I called every single person in my phonebook. The last person on my list was my gynecologist. I had no one else left.

He sent his nurse with the money.

I was scared sober and really angry. What would I do now? Nothing was working. I had tried everything: praying, counseling, and suicide. There was nothing left.

When I got home, everyone was sleeping. The glass had been cleaned up, but the floors were beginning to warp from the broken fish tank. The adrenaline was pumping even though it was 2 A.M. I stood there completely powerless over what to do. The only person that I trusted at this point was the counselor that I had been seeing. I called the emergency number. "Please call me back," I was thinking. It seemed to take forever. The drugs and alcohol were wearing off and I was shaking violently.

The phone rang. I answered it on the first ring.
"Rich, I'm in trouble."
"What's going on?"
"I have no one else to turn to. I wanted to kill my kids. I drank all day in order to get the courage to do it, because I can no longer handle the responsibility of taking care of them. I can't even take care of myself! I was desperate, but when I got home I couldn't do it because I was afraid of going to jail, so I broke all of the glass in my house. The tables, lamps even the fish tank, and now the floor is warped and coming up. I can't live like this. I want to die. No matter what I do, it doesn't work."

I felt like I was talking really fast, so he could come up with a solution that would work immediately!!!

"I think all of your problems are because you are an alcoholic and you need to go to AA." How did he know that? I had never told him that I drank. I could not accept that he labeled me as an alcoholic. I heard once, if one person tells you something about yourself, you don't have to pay attention. If two people or more tell you the same thing, God is trying to talk to you. This was the second person that said I was an alcoholic.

90

I hung up the phone without saying goodbye. I was numb. The clock stopped ticking. My world was at a standstill. I felt sick, not because of the drinking, but because I was looking back at my life. I was so full of pain and bad decisions. I was so unhappy. I could not go any lower. I was spiritually, mentally, and morally bankrupt.

I cannot describe the true helpless, hopeless feeling I had. My world was empty, dark, and completely void. I stood there paralyzed by fear. Fear of the unknown, fear of more bad decisions, fear of giving up everything that covered up the pain. I did not want to be me.

I had nowhere to turn. I had never heard of AA but if Rich said I should do it, I was willing to try anything. The only thing I could think was "my way wasn't working." I did not expect that anything would help; so far, I thought, I had tried everything. I had been doing it by myself, making all of my own choices. I was only thirty-three and in such a short adult life, I had screwed up everything by making bad choices.

I'm sure God was waiting for me to make the right choice, the one that would change me forever. Free will was not working.

CHAPTER 10
FINDING WHO I REALLY AM

TWELVE STEPS TO FREEDOM

I picked up the phone and called the 24-hour hotline to Alcoholics Anonymous. The answering service said they would have someone call me. A lady called me right back. By now it was about 6 A.M. The lady told me her story and the pain she had experienced until she quit drinking. I could not relate to her story but I could relate to the feelings. She asked if I wanted to go to a meeting in a couple of hours. I had no sleep and I was very hung over from drinking all day the day before. She asked me not to drink or do drugs until I went to the meeting. How would I stay awake without my amphetamines? It was October 11, 1977. I was afraid to go, but afraid not to. I agreed to try it one time.

Two ladies came to my house to pick me up. I had no idea what to expect. We got to the meeting which wasn't far from my house. When we walked in, everyone was laughing and seemed to be enjoying themselves. I was not laughing and was sure that I would never laugh again. I could not remember the last time I had laughed. Anger and sadness were my only emotions. The rest of the time, I was void. I did not have a good time drinking. I was not the life of the party. I was either standing behind a plant, crying, starting a fight, or fighting.

Since it was my first time, everyone told their story first. Then, it was my turn. They told me I didn't have to say anything but I thought I should, so they could tell me that I was in the wrong place. They didn't do that. They listened and then a couple of guys threw money on the table and bet that I would not make it.

Amidst all the commotion, there was something different about the place. It was very strange to me, like a world that I have never known before. As we finished the session, I stayed and looked at the room. It was simple, like a bland, undecorated meeting hall. The signs on the wall caught my attention. I walked toward them and read every step slowly, like a dream.

The Twelve Steps

STEP ONE
*"We admitted we were powerless over alcohol-
that our lives had become unmanageable."*

I wasn't sure that I belonged there. Maybe I was powerless over the first drink, but my life unmanageable? NEVER! I was fine. Didn't everyone live like I did?

They said I had to quit drinking and doing drugs one day at a time, and if I wanted to get better, I needed to go to ninety meetings in ninety days. I told them that would not be possible. I needed to work and take care of my kids. They told me I didn't have to do it, but it would be better if I did. I made a commitment to myself to try. My way hadn't worked. I was willing to follow any advice to feel better. I was blessed with the fact that I listened to this advice. I did not have any resistance left. I was beaten down to the ground.

At my second meeting the next day, I met a man and told him I was still not sure this was for me. He told me to try for thirty days and if it didn't work, they would happily refund my misery. He also told me that only three out of ten would make it. I made a commitment to myself to try it 100 % for thirty days. I thought if I did not see an improvement, I could always go back to doing it my way.

I wanted to be one of the three out of ten. Statistics show that today, it is two out of ten. My theory is that people today, go to treatment and are put on medication. Medication prevents you from feeling your true feelings so you never have to deal with the pain. I wanted to die, was in intensive care from suicide attempts, and would probably be diagnosed as a manic depressant or bipolar today. Those terms were not available were not available when I got sober. I still do not take ANY mood altering medication. Pain pills, cough medicine, anything that would threaten my sobriety. I want to deal with life on life's terms. God says he will never give me more than I can handle, and so far that has been true.

They told me I had to work the 12 steps, one at a time, so I could change. They said drinking was a symptom of the underlying cause; it is character defects that make us drink. The key is to find out what they are.

They also told me not to make any life changes for one year. I did not think it was very good trying to get sober living with a drug dealer, so that was the one thing I could not listen to. I went to look for an apartment, and once again the man I was living with told me I wouldn't make it. I had to! I was completely out of options.

STEP TWO
"Came to believe that a Power greater than ourselves could restore us to sanity.

You want me to do WHAT??? After all, God had abandoned me a long time ago. Where was he when I was abandoned by my mom, being beaten by my foster mom, and husband? I had no problem admitting my insanity, but a Power greater than myself? I would learn by hindsight that, "God was doing for me what I could not for myself." Slowly, things were beginning to change in spite of me.

I did attend my ninety meetings, in ninety days. The only difference I noticed was that people were getting nicer, but I was still not sure this was the way to go. This was really different. I noticed that I did not wake up wanting to die. I still did not want to live, but I did not want to die, and I no longer wanted to kill people. That was a start. I was now at Step Three.

STEP THREE
"Made a decision to turn our will and our lives over to the care of God as we understood Him."

I tried to stay in charge, but the only thing I could admit was my way wasn't working. I knew from my very being that if I did not do this as sincerely as I could, I would drink again. Willingness was the key, which I had none. I had to do this. Dependence was a means to independence. I had to let God be in charge, sit back, and wait and watch. Faith was not the problem; it was trust. Trust that it would turn out the way I thought it should, and trust that I would be able to accept that it might not be the way I thought it should.

It says in *How It Works* that, "half measures availed us nothing." I noticed after I had been sober six months, I was not doing as well as I should. Maybe it had to do with the fact that I kept a stash of pills in case I wanted to kill myself or the emergency joint in my wallet in case my kids got hurt and I couldn't handle it. I flushed the pills and my emergency joint. I had never been so scared. I had nothing to fall back on in case this didn't work.

When I got sober, I gave up the pills, drinking, and pot all at once. I shook violently for a year. It took a year to be able to hold a glass in one hand.

It was BORING! I WAS ADDICTED TO CHAOS! And excitement! I remember looking out of the window, thinking, "Is this all there is?" It was really hard to get used to.

Another hard thing to get used to was happiness. I had only experienced sadness. I went to a hypnotist to ask him to hypnotize me to remember a happy time in my life. There were none.

I had no idea what happiness felt like and was sure I would not like it. Then, we were at the fourth step.

STEP FOUR
*"Made a searching and fearless
moral inventory of ourselves."*

The inventory. No problem I had been going to counselors, looking at myself. This would be a piece of cake. I did not know how dishonest I was with myself and how all of my defects were nicely labeled. What I thought were my assets, turned out to be my liabilities.

Self centeredness? Not me. I just had to take care of myself. Fear? No way! If I ever felt fear, I would drink and it would be gone. And thank God, I didn't have pride. Certainly, no resentment about my mom abusing me or my real mom giving me away! I would get an "A" on my first 4th step.

Most alcoholics are driven by fear, fear that we will not get what we want or lose what we have. Problems with dishonestly, self centeredness, and resentment did not apply to me. It is like peeling an onion, layers and layers, and the willingness to look at my part. Self-justification is dangerous. It is so much easier to blame everything on someone else. That way, we don't have to accept responsibility for anything. Moral inventory, were they talking about me?

STEP FIVE
"Admitted to God, to ourselves, and to another human being the exact nature of our wrongs."

I had no trouble with the fifth step the first time, admitting my defects to another because my fourth step was so incomplete, and I could not see how dishonest I had been with myself. It took nine fourth steps and ten years to begin to see clearly that I had some serious defects. The last fifth step I did was the hardest. I had to seriously look at myself again. I had to admit that I still needed more work that would be constant for a lifetime. I have always considered my character defects to be in remission, just waiting to reappear. It is a process and the longer I am sober, the easier it gets to see my part and admit my shortcomings. I have always been plagued by fear. Fear that I would be abandoned by people I love. Envy of other people's families. Resentment toward my moms and step dad. I did not want to look at these defects, or work on them, so I buried everything until I knew I had to get honest or else I would drink again.

These were the hardest. I didn't want to tell myself, but I surely didn't want anyone else to know. I would have rather gone on pretending that everything was fine, but when I am discontent I need to look at myself because defects will make me drink again.

Now we get to the hardest part.

STEP SIX
*"Were entirely ready to remove
all these defects of character."*

It says that this is the step that separates "the men from the boys". The willingness to change. In the beginning it did not seem that I had that much to change. YET! They told me I had to be willing to give up ALL of those character defects, which were causing the problems. Addictions are the symptom of the underlying cause. It is our character defects that cause the problems and make us want to feed addictions such as alcohol, drugs, spending, gambling, and sex as outlets to cover up the defects. Addictive behavior is only a temporary solution to a permanent problem. When we wake up the next day, we realize we still have the same problems. I need to be willing to learn how not to react to my environment. When my character defects resurface or new ones appear I need to admit them and then become willing to take action and do something about them. This is really hard and requires constant vigilance and effort.

My goal is to TRY and be the best person possible, so that I never want to escape reality again.

STEP SEVEN
"Humbly asked Him to remove our shortcomings."

What does humbly mean? I had no idea. I didn't even like me, how could I be humble? Humility for me is admitting my powerlessness over, not only my drinking, but my character defects. Some of us have superiority attitudes, with an inferiority complex. It is our egos and selfish self-centered behavior that is at the crux of the problem. We need ego deflation.

When I finally surrender that I am powerless over my defects, I need to ask a Higher Power for help in alleviating them because I am not capable of doing it on my own.

I become humble, because I get out of the way.

STEP EIGHT
"Made a list of all persons we had harmed, and became willing to make amends to them all."

Had I harmed anyone? My arrogance and ego said no. This step was really hard for me, I thought I was the one that had been hurt by others, and I was not willing to forgive anyone. Little did I know that forgiveness is the key?

Forgiving the people that had harmed me, I think not. This would happen much later. It says we are constitutionally incapable of having relationships with others and this step would end our isolation with others and teach us how to be a friend. I did not have any idea how to have relationships with anyone. I would sooner walk away. I never wanted to work anything out because I was so afraid to tell anyone how I felt, because then I would be vulnerable.

When I joined AA, I was told in order to forgive my mom I needed to pray for her. I must say when I started praying it was not sincere, and never was. I did it because someone said that I should. Once again, I thought "It couldn't hurt." This one step has made the biggest difference in my life with relationships.

I finally realized that if I kept walking away and not resolving any problems, I would run out of people.

STEP NINE
"Made direct amends to such people whenever possible, except when to do so would injure them or others."

I had no problem saying "Sorry." It was quite clear I had not been a very nice person. This one is tricky; you do not want to tell someone that you had an affair with their husband, because it would hurt them. We need advice from our sponsor because most of us want to right every wrong. I had taken money from the dentist that I worked for. He had moved and I had no idea how to reach him so I wrote a check to charity. It was easy for me to accept responsibility for hurting people. Forgiving my moms, NEVER! Every time I thought about my mom, a knot would form in my stomach; I was willing to die with it. I would take my pain with me to the grave. I thought!

STEP TEN
"Continued to take personal inventory and when we wrong promptly admitted it."

Try to make things right before the end of the day. This requires constant examination of my motives. We can no longer justify our behavior. I cannot live with guilt and remorse. Did I hurt someone's feelings; did someone give me too much change? There is no such thing as justifiable anger, was I fearful and anxious? Was there anything that would cause me to be discontent? If so, it needs to be resolved? Unfortunately not everyone cooperates. My insecurity and fears still return. I require patience from my friendships, but I have true friends today. When I was drinking, I prided myself on how good I could lie to your face. No one ever suspected. I was cold and heartless. I didn't care if you liked me or not. If you didn't, I just found someone else.

100

Today, I am a child of God, trying to be the best I can be. I meet with failures and difficulty like everyone else. At least I am willing to take responsibility for my behavior today.

STEP ELEVEN

"Sought through prayer and meditation to improve our conscious contact with God, as we understood Him, praying only for the knowledge of His will for us and the power to carry that out."

It was easy for me to do the first half of this step. I have always prayed and meditated. I was sober seventeen years, when one day, I looked at the wall and saw the second half of this step. When did they put that in? Praying ONLY for the knowledge of his will and the power to carry that out. It's really easy when everything is going good, just the way you would like, with everything falling into place. But when we don't seem to get things the way we think they should be, we question. Sometimes I think God is reading the wrong script, He got me mixed up with someone else. "This isn't the way I wanted it to be," like a child throwing a tantrum. The real key to serenity is ACCEPTING things just the way they are, this second, this minute, without wanting it to be different. When I can do that, I am practicing humility. I do not know God's plan. It is all about trust. Faith has never been a factor. Trust has been an issue. We are convinced that happiness comes from getting what we want. We need pain and suffering to develop us and strengthen our faith. Weakness and helplessness is my strength.

I will never understand the plan and He doesn't need my help or direction. I can only ask for His will and wait to see what happens with peace and faith.

STEP TWELVE

"Having had a spiritual awakening as the result of these steps, we tried to carry this message to alcoholics, and to practice these principles in all our affairs."

In the program it says, "When anyone, anywhere reaches out for help, let the hand of AA be there." It is difficult to be available 24/7 for those phone calls of drunken people calling the answering service at 2AM. Trying to talk sense to a drunk, who is at their lowest point, definitely teaches patience and tolerance. I understand their despair. I tell them my story and ask if they want to go to a meeting. I will call in the morning to take them. Ninety-nine percent of these people never answer the phone the next day. It keeps me sober, because it reminds me where I was. Helping others and making ourselves available, by listening and taking them to meetings. One Thanksgiving eve, I sat with a lady all night and then checked her into the hospital. I had to cook Thanksgiving dinner with no sleep. I called in the morning to see how she was doing but she had checked out.

The second half of the step is the most difficult. Practice these principles in all our affairs? Good in theory, but really hard to do.

When I first came to AA, I had no idea what right and wrong was. I had never felt either and even if I did have a wrong feeling, I would drink it away or rationalize it. For a long time in AA, I could only feel what wrong was, but still never knew right. Today I know the difference.

* * * * * * * * *

Always trying to be what I know God wants me to be all day, every day, is really hard but is my mission. I fall and falter. I get hurt and sad. I question The Plan. Isolation is a problem for me and some people in AA. We want to sit alone and feel sorry for ourselves. It has been a process for me, asking people for help. I could have never done that before and sometimes I need a lot of reassurance. Those old tapes come back and say, "You need to give up." I have always been a passionate person and am a person of extremes. It is either the "best" or the "worst." It is a problem for people with addictions. I wanted to invent a game called "Worse Case Scenario." Most of us can take any topic and project it into the worst possible scenario. If my son was coming home late, by the time he got home, I had already convinced myself that he was dead in a cornfield, never to be found.

I have peace when I am helping others by getting out of myself, attending meetings, working at the food bank, or just being available to help anyone that needs help. I no longer want to isolate. I want to give back for the blessings that I have been given because of my program and faith. God has been good to me because I was willing to help myself.

I have the most difficulty in "practicing these principles in all of my affairs," with my family. Watching them with their addictions and problems in their life is the most difficult thing I have ever done. I still have remorse that I was not the parent that I could have been, and sometimes I am plagued with guilt. I understand the theory that I am powerless over their choices, but this issue causes me problems. I want everyone to have a wonderful life and not hurt the way I have hurt. So far, no one is cooperating, with what I would like to see for their life. The only way I deal with this is to accept their choices, my powerlessness, and continue to pray. God's will, not mine, be done.

* * * * * * * * *

I wanted to save the world. If I could get sober, everyone could. I wanted to be an alcoholism counselor right away; until someone asked me what I would do if someone committed suicide or went back to drinking. It took awhile for me to understand that not everyone wants to get sober. Many would die, go insane, or go to jail. It is a fatal disease.

The first day I came to the program, my compulsion to drink was lifted. I did not want to live in the hell that I had been living in. I think if people struggle with staying sober, they really do not want to quit. That is just my thought. I have always understood that I could drink if I wanted to; no one ever said I could not, but I clearly understand that I probably would not make it back. If anyone thinks they can go back to drinking then, come back when they don't want to drink anymore, they are taking a big risk. Most people never come back. I was not willing to take that chance. I was given a gift and would treat it with care. I did whatever I was told. I had no defense. I never said "just because it worked for you, doesn't mean it will work for me." I did whatever anyone suggested, because the only thing I could admit was my way wasn't working.

I have lost many, many friends to drinking, someone had a train accident, someone drowned in the shower, and someone slashed her wrist. The worst so far was the lady that let a car hit her while holding her baby. These are just a few, many suicides, people lying paralyzed in nursing homes, people in prison. It never has a good ending.

I understand the hopelessness and the pain. There is no such thing as just having one drink. If I knew I could drink and then come back to AA, I might consider that. But the real truth is you probably only have one recovery and eighty percent of people NEVER make it back.

I never miss my meetings and if I miss one of my regular days, I make it up that week. Even when I am out of town I go.   It keeps me on even keel with reality. I know I need a meeting when I am waiting in line and I want to run over you with my grocery cart. Even my granddaughters said that I needed a meeting when we were on vacation once. I was yelling about something. I did go, and had an immediate transformation. I do not know why it works, but you walk in feeling crummy and walk out feeling good.

For me, sobriety is life or death. Anyone can go to church and then go out and do whatever they want when they leave the church. For me, I feel I have to try and live the way God wants me to live and if I don't, I risk that I will drink again. I never want that pain back. One of our sayings is, "My worst day sober is better than my best day drunk."

My opinions on AA are purely my own and it is different for everyone. These are the principles I have tried to incorporate into my life.

My favorite reading says:

There seems to be a right way and wrong way to live. When you live the right way things seem to work out well. When you live the wrong way, things seem to work out badly. You seem to take out of life what you put into it. If you disobey the laws of nature, you will be unhealthy. If you disobey the spiritual and moral laws, chances are you will be unhappy. By following the spiritual laws of honestly, purity, unselfishness, and love, you can expect to be reasonably happy and healthy.

* * * * *

I read this every time I give a talk at a big meeting.   It sums everything up, the way it was, and the way it is now.

THE TRUTH ABOUT ALCOHOL

I drank for happiness and became unhappy
I drank for joy and became miserable
I drank for sociability and became argumentative
I drank for sophistication and became obnoxious
I drank for friendship and made enemies
I drank for sleep and awakened without rest
I drank for strength and felt weak
I drank "medicinally" and acquired health problems
I drank for relaxation and got the shakes
I drank for bravery and became afraid
I drank for confidence and became doubtful
I drank to make conversation easier and slurred my words
I drank to feel heavenly and ended up feeling like hell
I drank to forget and was forgotten
I drank for freedom and became a slave
I drank to erase problems and created more
I drank to cope with life and invited death

I AM MORE

I am more than happy, I am joyful
I am more than healthy, I am whole
I am more than alive, I am radiant
I am more than successful, I am free
I am more than caring, I am loving
I am more than tranquil, I am peaceful
I am more than interested, I am involved

I am more than adequate, I am triumphant
I am more than fortunate, I am prosperous
I am more than human; I am a child of God

Ryan, you will see even though I quit drinking, I did not have an immediate transformation. It has been a very long process, and I am still working on it. The world would be a better place if everyone would incorporate the twelve steps into their lives. I pray you will only become familiar with them reading like this, and not have to see them on the wall as I do, at an AA meeting.

CHAPTER 11
ABUSE WHILE SOBER

BLOOD STAINED DRAPES

Everything was going along well. Scott, my younger son, was in military school because he had a learning disability. He had been going to public school, but they locked him in a wooden box for asking for a Band-Aid at an inappropriate time. I called for a due process hearing, where I was my own lawyer. The school district admitted failure and sent my son to a local military school. He excelled in the structured environment.

My older son was graduating high school and decided he would join the Air Force. He was working at the pool, at our apartment complex. He was dating a girl, and thought he wanted to marry her. She moved back to live with her parents when he enlisted because she thought she would wait for him at home. By coincidence, he got stationed in her hometown; so, of course, as soon as he moved there, they made wedding plans. They married when he was nineteen. It was 1981.

For his 18th birthday, before he left for the Air Force, I had a party at the clubhouse. It was great. I invited all of my friends. There were people that told other people about the party. A man showed up that I had never seen before. I was not dating anyone and he got my attention. He was very attractive. Of course, I made my way to him. We talked for a while, when he asked me to come to his house for dinner. His name was Roger.

With one son only coming home on weekends and the other one going away, I only had to worry about me. I went to his house the following week. It had a wall of windows in the back of the house overlooking a beautiful yard. It was very impressive. I looked at all of his decorations. Everything was mesmerizing. I wouldn't change a thing. He had his own business and was obviously successful, if he could live in a house like this. Everything looked perfect, except for a blood stain on the drapes.

Roger made a wonderful steak, baked potatoes, and salad. This was perfect: a good looking man, a great house, and someone cooking dinner for me. He was really charming and had a great sense of humor. I needed to laugh more.

I asked about his life and he told me that he had divorced his wife because she was crazy. He said she was violent. I felt sorry for him; he deserved someone nice, like me. He asked if I would like to go away the following weekend. I hadn't gone anywhere since I took the kids to Disney, six years before. The only time I didn't have the kids was when they were at camp. I needed a break from all of the responsibility. I left my husband at twenty-five, and I was now thirty-six.

It sounded great to me. I was happy to go anywhere. Sure, I would love to. I got someone to watch my son, and I was off on a new adventure.

Roger and I had so much fun. He was also in AA, so we didn't drink. He took me to a really nice lodge and we had very romantic dinners. He would hold my hand and look into my eyes with the most beautiful blue eyes I had ever seen. My heart was melting. It was so nice to have this break.

On the way back home, out of the blue, Roger said, "I had a great time, why don't you come to live with me?" He was successful, good looking, and lived in a great house. Without hesitation, I said, "Sure!" I had known him a week.

I did not give it a second thought. I had never lived in a house before and this was a really nice house. Plus, he was so nice. This would work out just fine. I went home, sublet my apartment, and sold my furniture. I moved in the following week.

My cat had just had kittens so I had four cats.
"I don't like cats." Roger said. "Get rid of them."
"No, I can't do that."
"OK, I will allow you to keep two."

I missed the word ALLOW! I should have suspected something, but I was on a cloud. This was the answer to my prayers, a nice house and a nice man to take care of me. I really loved those cats, but I gave them away. I would never do that again. After being in the house just for a week, the abuse began.

I became the maid, he found fault with everything I did. The stove was not clean enough; the laundry wasn't done on time; I didn't vacuum well enough. No matter what it was, it was not good enough, and I am a good housekeeper. I tried really hard to please him so he wouldn't get angry.

When he got angry, which was most of the time, he would yell, and say the vilest, most vulgar things I had ever heard. No one had ever sworn at me before. My ex-husband was a mechanic, the man that broke my nose. Even he had never sworn in front of me. This was the first time I was being called the worst names you can call a woman. I knew what they meant. I had just never heard them in relation to me.

This, without exception, was the meanest person that I had ever met. Now, what do I do? I had nowhere to go, no apartment, and no furniture. I no longer drank, so there was nothing I could do to cover up the pain from the abuse.

He never hit me; I would have rather been hit. At least the cuts and bruises heal. This was worse. He was attacking my character. This was killing my heart and soul. Even my mom yelling had not hurt me this much. I was trapped again.

After these episodes of verbal abuse, he would become really nice and affectionate. He would hold my hand a look into my eyes with those beautiful blue eyes and get tears. He would be so sorry. He would buy me flowers and take me to nice places. Each time, I would believe it will not happen again. He was just in a bad mood. I made excuses for his behavior, and I tried harder to please him. I had been sober for four years. Wasn't I supposed to be capable of making good decisions? Maybe if I would have talked to someone about my decision to move in with someone that I had known for a week, I would not be in this position. I was back into self-will; I wanted to do this without any help or advice from anyone. I did not want anyone to try and change my mind. I had a sponsor that I should have confided in, but she never knew that I moved until it was too late.

As soon as I moved in, he said he would control the money so I had to give him my paycheck from the dentist. I had no money of my own; I had to ask him if I wanted to buy anything.

One day, I said. "I need money to buy a bra." How humiliating that I had to ask for money to buy personal items.

"You will have to save for it out of the grocery money," he retorted.

He did whatever he wanted but I was not allowed to do anything without his permission. I had to obey him or else he would get violent. I had to get out of there as quickly as possible. I had only been there about a month. Again, I needed a new plan. I started saving money out of the grocery money...

"YOU COULD SELL ANYTHING TO ANYONE""

A friend of ours, Rob, was the president of the largest health and beauty business in the country. One day we were talking and I told him I needed a different job; I needed to make more money. I could not tell him about the position I had gotten myself into with his friend. Working for the dentist, I was only making $10,000 a year. I had raised two boys on that and my rent alone was $4000. Now I had no money and I needed to make enough money to really take care of myself so I would not be poor when I left Roger. I was so tired of being poor. There were times we only had Kool-Aid and bologna in the fridge. I did not want to go back to that. Being poor fueled me to make a very bad decision.

Rob looked at me and without hesitation said, "You belong in sales."
"That's ridiculous. I do not know how to sell anything. I only went to ninth grade. I do not have any skills. No one would hire me!" I laughed, thinking he was joking.

"I would hire you, because you have street knowledge. That is better than an education for some sales people." He knew this because he had been poor and had to put himself through school, he then went into sales. I guess he could see something in me that I could not.

"I will write personal letters to the presidents of all of the major companies," Rob said. He also had me interview with his human resource person, who wrote a resume for me. Rob sent it to seventy-five of the largest companies.

I got interviews. I'm sure they were interviewing me out of consideration to Rob. I did not get any of the jobs. I thought Rob had no idea what he was talking about, when he said I should be in sales. Yeah, right! I was very discouraged. I would be stuck in hell forever. There was no hope.

* * * * * * * * * *

By now, people were telling me what really happened to Rogers's last wife. He had a violent fight with her and hurt her. That is why the blood was on the drapes. My husband beat me, now this. Every time Roger was abusive, I wanted to believe it would never happen again. I wish I would have known, a long time ago, that the abuse in any relationship will never stop. The only way to stop the abuse is to leave.

Ryan I did the same thing again. I kept moving in with people to make my life better. I needed to do that for myself first, in order to have healthy relationships. Healthy people do not choose unhealthy people. Get to know someone. NEVER move in with them before you marry. First, God doesn't want you to. Second, it puts the relationship on a casual basis. When people are married they will try really hard to make it work, because they do not want to divorce. When living together you just say, "If you don't like it, leave."

CHAPTER 12
THE REAL TURNING POINT

A LIFE-CHANGING EPIPHANY

The abuse went on and on. There were really good times, convincing me that it would never happen again, and then it would happen. Each time I got more and more depressed. Would I ever be able to get out? After three long years I had enough money saved from the grocery money to get out and get an apartment.

I went back to the ghetto and found a really nice apartment: once you got inside. I got more furniture. It was the winter of 1984 and I would soon be forty, starting over from scratch for the fifth time. I had to start anew when I left my first husband, then when someone robbed me and stole everything I owned, again when I left my second husband and then the drug dealer. Now number five. It was getting easier. God kept giving me the strength, and more chances. He must be very patient. I needed to start doing my part so this would never happen again.

BUT!! I kept seeing Roger, because Christmas and my birthday were coming. I did not want to be alone. I thought it would be better now since we were separated. He would notice how special I was and appreciate me. Then he would not be mean to me anymore. I was wrong again. What a painful lesson to learn. Never trust the abuser. He will not change.

It was Christmas Eve. I was standing at the stove cooking pork chops. I did not know what it was exactly, that agitated him. He kept saying really degrading things to me. "I don't know why I keep seeing you. You're a useless piece of s—t! You are just hopeless; you will never have anything or be anybody...

No wonder you are still single and no one wants you." I looked him right in those empty blue eyes. Something happened inside of me. I put down the fork that I was using to turn the pork chops and said to myself, "No one will ever treat me this way again. I will find a way NEVER to be dependent on someone to take care of me again."

I had an epiphany. This time, his words didn't hurt. I put on my coat and walked out of the door never to return again. I didn't know what I would do, but I knew what I wouldn't do. I would never allow anyone to hurt me again. I would find a way to take care of myself.

He never thought I would stay gone with Christmas and my birthday coming. I did not call and would not answer the phone.

For my birthday, two days after Christmas, Roger came to my apartment and proposed. He told me I needed him and I would never be able to make it on my own. He gave me a ring. I took it and told him I would consider it. I kept the ring and never talked to him again.

PRAYING FOR A THERMOSTAT

My apartment was in the ghetto, and I hardly made any money at the dentist, but I was grateful for what I had and for the strength to be away from Roger.

The difference was with me. I was now happy. Nothing had really changed. I was still poor. Everything was OK. I had accepted that I would be poor, and I was fine with it. I was still uneducated. I never went back to school because I had no one to help me with my kids. Plus, I didn't have an extra penny. I would look for better jobs every week in the paper, but then I would say "They will never hire me." I never pursued it farther. I had been sober seven years.

That winter of the week of Christmas of 1983 was among the coldest in the Midwest. The temperatures stayed at 20-25 below 0, even without the wind chill. The city was paralyzed by the cold. No one could go anywhere. Cars would not start, the oil was freezing.

It was so cold in my apartment that I had frost on my bathroom mirror. The apartment had heat, but it just wasn't enough. I lived on the third floor and the heat ran out before it got to my floor. The windows were leaking cold air. The only way to stay warm was to sit in front of the oven with the door open. It was Christmas.

I put my hands together and prayed, "God, please let me have a thermostat." This one prayer would change my life forever.

FINDING MY NICHE

Two weeks after I asked for the thermostat, a patient's dad came into the orthodontist office where I worked. He stopped by on a day when the dentist was not there to make a payment. He had seven kids. I had been there for fourteen years so I saw him frequently. I don't know why I told him I would like to make more money, and that I had no education or skills.

He said his company would be hiring 84 new people, because of a split with another company. He said I should apply and that they might hire me.

My two mottos when I came to AA were, "It couldn't hurt," and "What's the worst that could happen?" I didn't think they would hire me so I would go for the interview, and if I did and it didn't work out, "What was the worst that could happen?" I figured I could always go to work for another dentist.

I was more scared about taking the train for the interview than the interview. I had someone stay with me the night before for reassurance that I would be OK. I had never been on a train, and I was convinced that even if I got to downtown Chicago, I would get lost.

I went for the interview and was really early, because I compensated for the fact that I might get lost.

The first question they asked was, "Why should we hire you?" I didn't even have to think about it. I said, "Because you need me, and I need you." I would recommend this statement to anyone, since they hired me at that moment, on the spot.

Now what do I do? I was hired to sell. What if I couldn't do it? What if I didn't like it? Well, "What's the worst that could happen?" If I didn't try to get unstuck I would be stuck forever. I had no support system, no encouragement from anyone. I didn't think I could do it, but I had to try!!! I kept my dentist uniform and shoes, just in case I had to go back to work for a dentist.

We had six weeks of training. I asked more questions than anyone, plus I was never good at percentages, or any math. I thought I was in big trouble because there were things I didn't understand and others that I didn't want to do. I wanted to do it my way. I needed to compensate for what I couldn't learn. I have a learning disability but I knew I was smart. I needed to adapt the job to me, not the other way.

I was voted most likely to fail, but I will tell you, that out of the class of the 84 that they hired, I was the only one left standing after 22 years.

They gave us the worst of the worst to call. We had no idea what was good or bad, so I called everyone. We had accounts that spent up to $50 a month and our job was to increase it. It was new business, plus increase, minus loss.

I was never afraid to ask for an order. Once again, "All they can say is no." I had been there less than three months. They were paying us $3.00 for every dollar of net that we sold.

One day I got a hold of the right person to talk to about their business and I proposed that they spend $13,000.00 a month, instead of $19.50 a month and they took it!! I had to have a messenger service go get the signature because we did not have fax machines at that time.

By now the people on both sides of me had quit, and I was working their phones too. So now I had three phones. They would now let me do it my way, but would never let me mentor anyone.

I started looking for a place to buy. The dentist had given me $14,000 in profit sharing so I had the money to put down. I could get out of the ghetto forever. I would never be poor again. At the end of six months I had made $22,000.00 net, more than I could make for two years at the dentist.

The most important change was, I finally found something I was really good at. I had never been good at anything. All of my life, I considered myself a loser. Everyone that had ever been in my life had told me that many times and I believed them. Singing, dancing, art, sports, I wasn't good at any of them. I failed gym because I am totally uncoordinated. I even took tennis lessons and never hit the ball once. I had no education and no skills, or so I thought. I did not think I could do anything well. Selling was the gift God gave me. I just didn't know it and still wouldn't if I hadn't tried. This one thing has made the biggest difference in my life.

You do not have to believe in yourself, and you will never be sure. You just have to try. A counselor told me once, "Do something even if it's wrong." I was paralyzed by fear and indecision. I had hundreds of REAL reasons why I should stay stuck in poverty. Now, because I tried and never gave up, I had a chance to change the course of my life forever.

My new job had a ranking report that came out every week. It showed everyone in the company, based on performance for the week. After my sale, I got the weekly ranking report, and I was at the top. I made a decision at that moment; I would always be at the top.

I was not only good at this; I wanted to be the best!

I would go on to win the "Rookie of the Year" award, after being voted most likely to fail. "I WAS NOT HOPELESS!!"

CHAPTER 13
THE DAYS WHEN FLOWERS BLOOMED

A REALLY DIFFERENT LIFE

It was February and I had been working at my job for a few weeks. I had to take the train, and then a bus to my office. One day, I got off of the bus and there was a man named Paul, which I had known for years. Paul happened to be a really good friend of Roger.

He was walking with his head down and I said, "Lift up your head and shout it's going to be a great day."

He looked at me with a strange look on his face. His sad blue eyes were distant. I looked back at him and, without words; I was trying to say, "You look so unhappy. I bet I could make you happy."
"Hey, what are you doing downtown? I thought you worked for the dentist…" he asked.
"I just started a new job selling in this building," pointing at the building.
He had an office exactly across the street from my new office.
"How about lunch?" Paul said.
"I would love that. It's good to know someone down here, so I don't feel alone."
We had lunch in a really nice restaurant and got caught up on the latest news. We had known each other for about five years. We associated with all the same people and went to the same parties. I knew his wife, where he lived. We were friends.

There were things to talk about immediately. We laughed about my relationship with Roger and how that relationship had prompted me to get a new career.

Paul was a lawyer, and had been a doctor, but didn't like it. After he was married with children he went to law school. He was the most intelligent, educated man I had ever met. I was in awe of his intelligence.

He started calling me every day at my office to encourage me. When I was feeling down and did not want to do my job anymore, I would call him and he would say, "When it gets too tough for the other guys, it's just right for us," then he would send me flowers to cheer me up.

We had never really talked other than when we were at someone's house or at parties, so we never had real conversations. We really enjoyed talking to each other and agreed to meet every day for lunch. It was fun. I never saw him as a man, just a friend that I respected and he seemed to respect me. He would tell me I was the smartest person he had ever met and how much he believed in me. He encouraged me to keep on trying when it got hard. I never had anyone that believed in me. The day I got my big sale, he sent me flowers and asked me to dinner to celebrate. I thought that was so nice. I had never had anyone be kind this kind to me.

One day, Paul called and said he could not make lunch, because his biggest client was coming in. I told him if he really cared about me, he would have lunch with me. He left his client in his office and came for lunch.

THE MAN OF MY DREAMS

This relationship went on like this until June. One Sunday morning, there was a knock on my door. When I opened it Paul was standing there wearing leather chaps and a leather jacket.

Wow! He looked GREAT! He had ridden his motorcycle to my house. I had never seen him in casual clothes before. He looked different than the man that I had been having lunch with in the custom suits, with the monogrammed cuffs and cuff links.

He stood in the hall and said, "I have enjoyed every minute that we have spent together and I want to be with you all of the time. I want to have a real relationship with you."

I was in awe that a person of his stature and success would be interested in someone like me. It was a new feeling for me to feel good about myself and this was "really" different. He wanted ME!

We had talked about every aspect of his life and I knew how unhappy he was at home. I could not resist. I was sure I could make him happy.

From that day in June, we were never apart. He came over every day after work for dinner. It was like he didn't have a wife. Sometimes we would talk about it but it didn't seem to bother him. I could not understand why his wife was not causing a problem. He said as long as she had money it didn't matter.

He had inherited millions from his dad and said they would never divorce. I had no guilt. It seemed so right. He was everything: my prince, my knight, and the first man that ever that respected me and made me feel good about me. Even though I had promised myself that no one would ever get to my heart, it was too late. I had no defense. It happened in spite of me, because my guard was down.

Paul knew everything about me and still loved me. He gave me everything emotionally. He believed in me No one had ever done that before. He told me I could give him the feelings he was not getting at home and how much he wanted to be with me forever, but he would never be able to divorce his wife. I didn't care, as long as he was with me every waking minute.

What was I doing? He was married with three children. I could do this when I was drinking, but now I have been sober seven years. How could I live with myself? I would not even consider doing this today, but at that time it seemed so right. I needed his support for confidence to do my job, and as strange as it seems, I feel he was in my life to help me. I needed someone to lean on.

* * * * * * * * * *

Paul hated that I smoked, but with all of the stress of the job, I could not quit.

In July, my voice got hoarse. I thought I had been talking too much or had some virus. I went to the doctor and he told me to go see a throat specialist that day. I thought the doctor was exaggerating, but I did it. He said I had precancerous polyps on my larynx, and I had to have surgery a soon as possible.

They did it the next day. I had been smoking for twenty-five years. The day I had the surgery, I went back to smoking again. I was sure I would be OK. I could not talk for a month, because of my larynx. I found out if you can't ask for what you want; no one pays attention to you. How could I do my job, if I couldn't talk?

A year to the day, the polyps came back. This time they were not cancerous. God was going to give me one more chance to get it right. I knew that if I didn't quit they would take out my larynx. Another surgery, but this time I quit.

* * * * * * * * * *

Paul and I had a wonderful life. He belonged to the theatre. We went to concerts and went out for dinner almost every night. Cost was no object. We did everything together. His wife did not exist, for me or for him.

In September, we went on a motorcycle trip. He told his wife he had a business trip. It was great. His wife never wanted to do these things with him; he had opened up a whole new world for me. I had never been so happy. Not once did it seem wrong.

We had all of the same friends, and I would hear things that his wife said about him and tell him, to reassure him that he was doing the right thing by being with me. My best friend was also a friend of his wife. She certainly did not approve, but I didn't care.

On Thanksgiving he sent his family to Florida, so he could be with me. He told his wife he was too busy to go. She would be gone a week. It didn't matter when she was here; he was never with her anyway.

Paul took me to his house to show me where he lived. I still had no guilt. He belonged to me. We were both getting something that we needed from each other.

HOW WILL I LIVE WITHOUT YOU?

He was supposed to come for Christmas Eve. The phone rang. "I'm calling from home." Ok, his wife must be out, I thought. "My wife found out about us." Ok, she doesn't want you anyway, I said to myself.

124

"I can't see you anymore. She wants a divorce and there is too much money involved."

WHAT? I could not breathe. I could not talk. Was this his idea of a joke? His next sentence was going to be that he was kidding. He didn't say anything more.

He was everything to me; I did not think I could live without him in my life. He was the first and only person I really let see who I was and let into my heart. This was the only time I had ever been happy in a relationship. I needed him to survive. I didn't realize it at the time, but I was completely emotionally dependant on this man. More than I had ever been before because this was the first time I loved someone with my whole heart. Years and years of emotional insecurity, no real love. I was not capable of taking care of myself emotionally at this time.

I had my son call him at his house; I had to talk to him. He could not leave me.

He answered the phone. My son handed me the phone.
"Please, please do not do this to me," I begged.
"My decision is final." That was the only thing he said, and hung up the phone.

What could I do? There was no way to reach him. Those were years before cell phones, text, or email. The city had shut down for the holidays. I could not even show up at his office.

Sometime during the week after Christmas, he called.
"I've left my wife and I'm living in a hotel, until I find a place."
"I can't live without you, and I will file for divorce so we can be together forever."

LIVING THE LIFE

Finally at forty one, my life would be happy. I would have everything that I ever wanted: security, love, and someone that believed in me. I was totally dependent on him for my survival. I kept falling into the same pattern of dependence.

The following week, Paul bought a condo, paying cash so he could move in immediately. It was fun shopping for his condo, knowing that we would be together forever.

I was still living in my apartment waiting for the perfect place, so I could have my thermostat. A year and a half had gone by and I wanted to find a place before another winter. I didn't know what I wanted, because I had never had the option of having anything.

I had two promotions already and was financially secure for the first time. I was making four times more than I had at the dentist. I had a new car, and could furnish my new place. I would not have to worry about money ever again.

My friend who was a realtor found a condo for me. The strange thing, it was right across the street from Paul. It was all a coincidence. My living room window faced his bedroom. I took the condo because it was a really good deal. It had been a foreclosure and needed some cosmetic repair. It was beautiful, had three bedrooms, and had a sunken living room with a fireplace. Every room faced a lake, about 40 yards away. If anyone would have told me a few years before that I would move from the ghetto to this beautiful place, I would have laughed. I got my thermostat. It was from God. I prayed out of desperation, but I did not expect He would answer so soon and give it to me this way. He gave me more than a thermostat; He gave me a chance to find my niche and the thermostat was going to be my reminder of His goodness.

Every time I walk past my thermostat today, I am so grateful. I think everyone should be poor at least once to learn what really has meaning.

I had a great job, the man of my dreams, and now my very own condo. Could my life be more perfect?

We would fly to Mexico for the weekend. For Christmas, his kids could buy whatever they wanted for their family. I will never forget the whole living room filled with gifts. If we went to a record store he would buy one of everything. I was afraid to say I liked something because then I got it. I never got used to his excess. His kids liked me because they knew he had been so unhappy at home. Everything was going to be great. He would be divorced and we would be together forever.

The divorce was going through. I was called for a deposition, because his wife thought he had bought my car and condo. She knew me when I was poor and had no idea that I was now making money or that I had changed jobs. I proved that I had purchased everything by providing earnings and proper papers. She was shocked and had no idea that I was making what was considered good money for a woman twenty-five years ago. I'm sure she wanted me to burn in hell, but I felt the victor. I had her husband and she didn't.

He bought me a fur coat. I bought him a mink lined leather jacket and a Grandfather clock. I could now be financially independent. I wish I could have been emotionally independent. I did not know how to love or be loved. This was all new to me.

My life revolved around my job and my relationship with Paul.

MOTHER PAINS

Even though I was happy, my youngest son Scott was starting to have some serious problems. The chances of an alcoholic having children with the disease are 98 to 1. The best way to explain it is, if one or both of my parents drank and I didn't, I would still have the alcoholic personality. It travels through the family because even if no one drinks anymore, it is not a drinking problem; it is a thinking problem. Drinking is just a symptom of the underlying cause: our character defects. Most people in my life have come from alcoholic families. We seem to act and think differently. My counselor said I could scan a room and pick out the most dysfunctional person. They are fun. Maybe it is the sense of humor we had to develop to overcome the pain. Plus, some people that come from alcoholic families seem to be addicted to excitement.

I discovered my son had a drug problem when he was fourteen. I had no idea what to do. I went to a program that told me to lock him out and let him suffer consequences. I couldn't do it.

He got stabbed in the neck with his own knife and wound up on intensive care. While I was at work one day, his drug dealer came to my house and threw plants all over my living room and put jelly on the walls. Shrimp were stuck to the ceiling and orange juice was on the carpet. (I ran into this guy at AA meeting years later.)

Scott's lifestyle was putting such a strain on my relationship and my job. One day I got a call from the police saying my son had been arrested for a hit and run. I stopped breathing. I asked what had happened. The officer said my son hit a tree and drove off. I started laughing. They made me go to the station because I wasn't taking it seriously. I was just glad he hadn't killed someone. I would ground him and punish him, but nothing worked. The problems kept coming.

GOD TOOK IT AWAY

One day Scott came home covered in blood. He had gotten beaten by the police because they caught him drinking behind a store. When they put him in the police car, he tried to kick out the windows.

When I saw him, I said, "I need a cigarette." I went back to smoking. I had quit for five years after the surgery. Now, I was back full force. I tried counting my cigarettes, smoking half, everything. This time I did not want to quit. I was willing to die smoking. I remember lying on the couch, telling God I did not want to quit.

The next day, I was really sick; my throat was like raw meat. I could not swallow. I called in sick. I never called in sick. I remember looking at the clock at five in the afternoon and I realized I had not smoked. I never smoked again. God removed my desire to smoke, even when I didn't want Him to. He was always in charge. I knew I had a miracle in spite of myself.

GRAND MACCA

My older son Jim had been married for four years and everything seemed fine, except his wife told me he was drinking a lot. They were ready to have their first child.

It was going along OK for a couple of years, until my son had a very bad car accident. They did not have car insurance and it was his fault. The cost was $6,000; they did not have a penny. He got an additional job. The stress of not having any money, two jobs, and his drinking caused the marriage to fail. They decided to separate and get a divorce when my granddaughter was three. After they got divorced, right before he was moving to California, they decided to have sex to celebrate his birthday. His wife got pregnant, but even that was not enough to make him stay.

That was the only time I ever really wanted to drink again was the day he was leaving his pregnant wife and my granddaughter. His daughter was standing in the living room with her arms outstretched, saying, "Daddy, please don't leave." My heart was broken again, and I could do anything to help.

I left their apartment and went to a bar. As I was walking across the street, I thought," I don't know anyone in there." I had been sober eight years. It says in our book, there will come a time when you are incapable of not taking the first drink. This was my time. Thank God I had gone to a meeting the night before. I was being protected. I did not go into the bar.

I went to a travel agency and planned a trip to Disney for my granddaughter. I was trying to bring a little joy into her life to help her deal with the pain of losing her dad.

Seven months later, I took my daughter-in-law to the hospital to deliver my second granddaughter. Her dad, my son, was not there.

* * * * * * * * *

My relationship with Paul was great and I tried not to let what was going on with my family affect our life together.

One day, he sent enough flowers to my office to fill up the conference room table. There were roses, daisies, lilies, stargazers... a florist was in my office! He got down on his knees and asked me to marry him. I said NO. Everybody in the office could not believe I didn't accept his proposal. I was too afraid that if he loved me, he would eventually leave me. Just like Lock abandoned me.

My job couldn't be better. I was now making seven times more than the dentist and had three promotions. I always tried to be at the top of the ranking report. It was how I got my self-worth. It was visual proof that I was really capable of being good at something. Insecurity was ingrained in me. I was very successful in sales, because I was honest. I never sold something to someone that I didn't think they needed, and against the company, I did it my way. It's a good thing I was at the top. When you are at the top, you can do whatever you want. I won wonderful trips: Hawaii, Florida, a cruise. It was wonderful and first class. There was no going back. You can't stay at the Red Roof, when you have stayed at the Four Seasons. Money would never be a problem again.

Despite all of the great things going on in my life, there was something deep within that was missing and I still could not pinpoint what it was. There was some void there that was sucking my joy from being complete. I still did not feel whole and I had to find out why. As the commotions in my life came to a calm, I began to hear the voice of my childhood asking the question, "Who am I?" I could hear it at night, before I fell asleep. I could hear it in my waking hours, before the first hush of dawn.

Deep within, I knew what to do to find the answer.

CHAPTER 14
SEARCHING FOR MY ROOTS

MY REAL MOTHER

I realized that I was not just doing this for me. Ryan, I was also doing it for you and for the rest of our family, in order to give us all some roots, some sense of history, some clear sense of belongingness to a lineage. It does make a difference when you know where you have come from.

I had no idea who I was. What was my nationality? Why did my mom give me away? Why didn't she want to keep me? It was time for me to find out. I needed to know. I found a surge of energy inside me when I decided to look for my real mom.

I knew her maiden name and her hometown. I hired a detective agency and called everyone with that name in all of the surrounding towns. Nothing!

All of my adult life, I had envisioned meeting my real mom. I would finally hear a mom tell me that she loved me. I would finally get the nurturing I never had. I would feel worthy and secure for the first time because of my mom's approval.

Paul and I went to San Francisco, one summer for a vacation. We were passing through my real mom's hometown. That was one of the few things that I knew about her that stayed with me through these many years, thanks to Lillian. As we were driving, I saw the courthouse. I had a feeling. "Stop!" I said. Paul did not ask why.

I went in and asked if they had anything under her maiden name, Claire Blodgett. They had her marriage license. It was over forty-three years old, the same age as me. I looked at the names of the witnesses on the back. I went to the pay phone and looked in the telephone directory. Their names were listed.

Shaking, I called the number in the telephone directory. I begin by telling them my name. "I was passing through this town and I am trying to find someone that was from this town a long time ago."
"I think you know her. I see you stood up for her wedding." I told them how I found their name on the back of the marriage license.
"Her maiden name was Claire Blodgett."
"Why do you want to find her?" the lady asked.
"I am her daughter."

I heard the lady gasp on the other line. No one ever knew Claire had a child.
I explained that I wanted to meet her and ask about my birth.
"I will tell you what I know, but you have to promise never to tell her that we told you how to find her." I never told my mom, no matter how many times she would ask.

My imagination told me that Loretta Young was my mom and when I found her she would come down a spiral staircase wearing a long evening gown.

1 PLACE OF MARRIAGE
COUNTY OF SAN MATEO

STATE OF CALIFORNIA
Department of Public Health
VITAL STATISTICS
STANDARD CERTIFICATE OF MARRIAGE

State Index No.

Local Registered No. **620**

GROOM — PERSONAL AND STATISTICAL PARTICULARS — BRIDE

GROOM	BRIDE
2 FULL NAME WILLIAM JOHN CASEY	**14 FULL NAME** CLAIRE ELIZABETH BLODGETT
3 RESIDENCE 225 San Luis Ave. Lomita Park, Calif.	**15 RESIDENCE** 1346 El Camino Real Burlingame, Calif.
4 COLOR OR RACE White	**5 AGE AT LAST BIRTHDAY** 29 (Years)	**16 COLOR OR RACE** White	**17 AGE AT LAST BIRTHDAY** 23 (Years)
6 SINGLE WIDOWED OR DIVORCED Single	**7 NUMBER OF MARRIAGE** 1st	**18 SINGLE WIDOWED OR DIVORCED** (Annulment) Single	**19 NUMBER OF MARRIAGE** 2d
8 BIRTHPLACE Miles City, Montana (State or Country)	**20 BIRTHPLACE** Santa Cruz, Calif. (State or Country)
9 OCCUPATION (a) Trade, Profession or particular kind of work Clerk	**21 OCCUPATION** (a) Trade, Profession or particular kind of work Secretary
(b) General nature of industry, business, or establishment in which employed (or employer) Dalmo Victor Inc.	(b) General nature of industry, business, or establishment in which employed (or employer) Link Belt
10 NAME OF FATHER William J. Casey	**22 NAME OF FATHER** Orrin S. Blodgett
11 BIRTHPLACE OF FATHER Miles City, Montana (State or Country)	**23 BIRTHPLACE OF FATHER** Santa Cruz, Calif. (State or Country)
12 MAIDEN NAME OF MOTHER Muriel Stevenson	**24 MAIDEN NAME OF MOTHER** Mildred S. Hessey
13 BIRTHPLACE OF MOTHER Medford, Wisconsin (State or Country)	**25 BIRTHPLACE OF MOTHER** California (State or Country)

26 MAIDEN NAME OF BRIDE, IF SHE WAS PREVIOUSLY MARRIED

We, the groom and bride named in this Certificate, hereby certify that the information given therein is correct, to the best of our knowledge and belief.

William J Casey **27 Groom**   Claire Elizabeth Blodgett **28 Bride**

29 Filled out in the presence of Tillie Chiolero _____ Deputy County Clerk.

30 CERTIFICATE OF PERSON PERFORMING CEREMONY

I HEREBY CERTIFY that William John Casey and Claire Elizabeth Blodgett were joined in Marriage by me in accordance with the laws of the State of California, at Burlingame this 2nd day of July, 1944

31 Signature of Witness to the Marriage Houston F. Gafford
Signature of Person Performing the Ceremony Albert R. Kurtz

Residence San Carlos, Calif.   Official position Lutheran Minister

32 FILED JUL 5- 1944   T. C. Rice   Residence Burlingame, Calif.
Edith Betts, Deputy

A full, true and correct copy of the original recorded this _____ day of _____ 1944

_____ County Recorder.   By _____ Deputy.

The foregoing document is a true and correct copy of the original record filed in this office.

CERTIFIED   Dated: SEP 29 1996

Marvin Church, County Recorder in and for the County of San Mateo, State of California.

By _____ Deputy   #2379

134

342

VOL. _____ PAGE _____

STATE OF CALIFORNIA   MARRIAGE LICENSE   **COUNTY OF SAN MATEO**

THESE PRESENTS ARE TO AUTHORIZE and license any Justice of the Supreme Court, Justice of the District Courts of Appeal, Judge of the Superior Court, Judge of the Municipal Court, Justice of the Peace, Judge of any Police Court, City Recorder, Priest or Minister of the Gospel of any denomination, to solemnize within said

County the Marriage of_____**WILLIAM JOHN CASEY**_____, native of _____**Miles City, Montana**

aged____**29**____years, RACE OR COLOR ____**White**____, resident of _____**Lomita Park**_____, County of

_____**San Mateo**_____, State of _____**California**_____, and _____**CLAIRE ELIZABETH BLODGETT**

native of ____**Santa Cruz, Calif.**____, aged ____**23**____years, RACE OR COLOR ____**White**____, resident of

_____**Burlingame**_____, County of ____**San Mateo**____, State of ____**California**

The duly verified written consent_____to the issuance of this license to the above named minor_____ha_____ been presented to and filed by me.

IN WITNESS WHEREOF, I have hereunto set my hand and seal, this__**29th**__day of__**June**__, 19__**44**

W. H. AUGUSTUS
County Clerk and Ex-Officio Clerk of the Superior Court   By _____*Tillie Chisler*_____
in and for the County of San Mateo, State of California.   Deputy.
[SEAL]

(This License May Be Used at Any Time But Only in the County of San Mateo.)

STATE OF CALIFORNIA   CERTIFICATE OF MARRIAGE   **COUNTY OF SAN MATEO**

ORIGINAL

I HEREBY CERTIFY that on the____day of____*July*____, 19__44

at *Grace Lutheran Church, Burlingame* in the County of San Mateo,

State of California, under authority of a license issued by the County Clerk of said County, I, the undersigned, as a

Lutheran Minister joined in marriage *William John Casey*

and *Claire Elizabeth Blodgett* in the presence of *Harold J. Safford*

a resident of *San Carlos*, County of *San Mateo*

State of *California*, and *Lorraine C. Safford*, a resident

of *San Carlos*, County of *San Mateo*

State of *California*, who witnessed the ceremony *Herbert R. Kuntz*
Signature of Person Solemnizing Marriage.

JUL 5 - 1944   **181624**

Any officer or person who fails, neglects or refuses to perform any of the duties imposed upon him under the law concerning the registration of marriages shall be deemed guilty of a misdemeanor and punished in the same manner as other misdemeanors. (Sec. 3082 Political Code.) See information on margin.

Original, Filed for Record_____County Recorder, by_____Deputy.

This is the marriage certificate that I got from the courthouse. This was the key to finding Claire, and unlocking the mysteries of my life.

135

WHERE IS LORETTA YOUNG?

We went right to her house. I was shocked. She lived in a regular neighborhood, in an old ranch style house. No spiral staircase here, but she would be beautiful. I would surprise her and she would be so happy to finally find me. When she answered the door, it was like being zapped into the Twilight Zone. This definitely was not supposed to be this way! She was OLD!! Wrinkled and sloppy, she did not look anything like Loretta Young; she looked like me, only OLD. She had miles and miles of wrinkles, shallow blue eyes, and her hair was white. She had on dirty clothes and her teeth and fingernails were dirty. Please God, tell me that this will not happen to me!

"Yes, what can I do for you?" Claire said. At least she was polite.

"I'm your daughter." I thought she was going to have a heart attack. She couldn't speak and she was expressionless, but I knew she was not glad to see me. Not the reunion you see on TV when people reunite for the first time.

Her husband Bill, my step dad, was standing by her side. He looked like he was glad to see me. "Come in," he said, with a slight smile.

I was shocked at her living conditions. There was not one inch of space that didn't have something on it. She pushed everything aside on the table and asked if I wanted something to drink.

"No, thank you." I was afraid it would not be clean.
Claire, Bill and I all sat down at the table. There was awkward silence. We just looked at each other not knowing what to say

next. I thought I might as well ask the question that had plagued me all of my life.

"Did you ever try to find me?" I was sure the reason that she had not been able to find me was that Lillian had moved to another town, and remarried.

"No." She said emotionless, without taking the time to think about it. Since my birthday is at Christmas, if I had given a child away, whenever I heard Christmas songs, I would have missed my child and wondered how she was.

"I wanted to find you, but she didn't!" Bill said, pointing to my mom. "I always wanted a child and I wanted to know all about you. Every time I suggested that we look for you, she would stop me."

She had met him at work and got married to him seven months after returning home, seven months after I was born. Her mom had died three months before and probably would not have approved. This might have been the first independent decision that Claire made. She was never able to have any other children.

I had scripted this moment in my mind. My mom would start crying and grab me. She would tell me how much she loved and missed me. She would describe all the pain and regret she had for not finding a way to keep me.

I rephrased the question in another way, hoping it would be different: "Did you miss me or wonder what had happened to me?"

"No, not really. I had a very good life without you." She said without hesitation or feeling. I wish she would have made something up. I was not prepared for her answer. All of the longing that I had felt all those years was killed by that statement. I heard my foster mom saying, "I don't want you and your real mom didn't want you either," and now this coming from my real mother's mouth. It was hard to swallow. When Lillian, my foster mom, had said that my real mom didn't want me, I was sure that she was wrong. She wasn't wrong.

Then to make things as bad as they could possibly be, she took out photo albums and showed me her trips to Australia and Hawaii, to prove she had a wonderful life without me. I guess you can afford to travel more if you don't have kids.

I remember thinking who would have been a worse mom, the one that physically abused me or the one who gave me away because she didn't want me. These were the moms that God gave me? I did not understand. It's horrible to feel totally unloved by your moms; you would think out of two, I could have had at least one that was good. I left there promising to stay in touch but this lady would NEVER get a piece of my heart. Whatever she did from this point on, would not make a difference.

The empty heart that I came with was even emptier. I would go through life never feeling a mom's love. I think this is the source of my insecurity today. I still have trouble trusting when someone says they love me. I would go through life feeling unsure. The people in my developmental years never once told me that I was loved. I mourn for that little girl; she just wanted to be loved.

Ryan, you have filled that empty space that I have carried. God has expressed his true love for me, by giving you to me.

CHAPTER 15
A DEEP, DARK ABYSS

USED UP THE QUOTA

I had been in AA for nine years and had stopped working the steps because my life appeared to be going so well. I had a great job, the perfect man, and a beautiful place to live. I thought I had been cured. Isn't that what was supposed to happen? You get cured then you just have to go to meetings to help other people have what you have? I was going to teach them how to be character defect free, just like me. I would get up in the morning, have my quiet time, say the 3rd step prayer, turn my life and will over to God, then do whatever I wanted. If you liked it, fine. If you didn't, I didn't care. My life was perfect and I didn't need friends or the effort to be a nice person.

Then things started changing in my relationship. I noticed some emotional distance and I began to suspect Paul was seeing someone else. Remember my living room window faced his bedroom. We were going to be married as soon as the divorce was final, right?

"I feel that something is not right. Are you seeing someone else?" I said, not wanting to hear the answer.
"My wife was the only other woman I had been with other than you, and I wanted to be sure before we got married."
"I have been seeing someone for awhile, but she doesn't mean anything to me," Paul said. "I am so sorry; I will never do it again."
I wish I could have been more understanding. He had abandoned me, just like Lock. (I did not know I had this subconscious feeling until years later. It would sabotage my relationship.)

On New Year's Eve, I told Paul I was done with him. A man had moved in across the hall. His name was John. He was really cute and single. I knocked on his door. When he answered, I introduced myself and asked his name.
'Hi!" I said fearlessly.

"Since you're new to the neighborhood, if you are not busy, I said, how about we spend New Year's Eve together?" I was going to get even with Paul for hurting me.

"Sure." He said.

I had taken my keys back from Paul, so he could not get into my building. Paul rang and rang my bell, he could not get into the building, and he could not get back into my heart. I looked out of my window, and he was standing there with what seemed like ice on his teary eyes. Just like Dr. Zhivago. I laughed. I'll show him how it feels to be rejected.

I asked John, if he wanted to go to Key West with me, when he came over for New Year's. We left the next day. He was nice enough and really good looking, but I didn't like him, even a little bit. I was hurt. The man of my dreams had been seeing someone else. I would get even.

I trusted Paul with my heart. I gave him everything that was inside of me. I was not prepared to work this out. I could never trust him again. I was just too scared. The barriers were up. He would never get back into my heart; I had let my guard down for the first and last time. We kept going back and forth for the next five months. When he was gone, I would agonize about him, and when he was there I was so unsure, and scared he would hurt me. The abandoned girl never grew up.

After all, I did not know how to have a relationship, I NEEDED him. No one should ever depend on someone else for their happiness.

Looking back on this, after all of these years, I would have handled all of this differently. I know after a lot of counseling that I played a big part in all of what was going on. I had serious abandonment issues, because when I asked my step dad to help me, he told me to go away. I did not have any skills on how to deal with these kinds of things. No man other than the older man had ever left me. I thought, if you loved me, you would leave, so I would leave first.

I had been engaged eight times, and married twice. I think I used up my quota.

WHAT IS NORMAL?

I needed to focus on what was going on in my house. Scott had a drug problem and I was smart enough to know that he did not want to get help, so I felt my only choice was to lock him into a psych ward. I did not know it, but once he got in he could not be released without a court order. He needed to get help. He did not want it, but I thought it would work. I felt I had no other options. Codependency means that you care more about the problem than the person that has the problem. I wanted Scott to give up the drugs.

That same week, I was stopped on the road, trying to turn, and someone ran into the back of my new car totaling it out. Almost the same day, my office caught on fire and had to be closed. I had just ended my relationship with the man I loved, because he had been seeing someone else. It was the holidays.

I needed friends to help with my loss and problems. I had a multitude of problems and no one to turn to. I needed advice, but my friends were on the backburner, because I didn't need them when my life was perfect. Even today, I still have to ask advice because I do not know what NORMAL is. I thought it was a selection on the washing machine.

I was not prepared because I had stopped working the steps. Now what would I do? I had replaced God and my friends with my job and Paul.

I did not want to drink, but I felt crazy. I was desperate and lower than I was when I came to the program ten years earlier. I needed help, and I needed to mean it.

AND GOD SAID...

One day, shortly after, I was getting ready for work. Freezing rain was hitting the windows. I looked in the mirror and said," God why are things the way there are?" I heard a clear voice say, "Things are the way they are supposed to be, or else they would be different." I understood, for the first time that God was in charge and I had to step aside. It had to be a conscious decision. If I wanted what God had, I had to "Let go, and let God," lead the way.

I got down on my knees and asked God for help. I told God I would do whatever it takes. It was a life changing moment. From that day on, when I ask God for help, and say the 3rd step prayer:

God I offer myself to Thee-- to build with me and to do with me as Thou wilt. Relieve me of the bondage of self, that I may better do Thy will. Take away my difficulties, that victory over them may bear witness to those I would help of Thy Power, Thy Love and Thy Way of life. May I do Thy will always!

I have to mean it and try to live it. Does it always work? NO! It is a lifetime process. This was the beginning of my genuine spiritual life.

FILLING THE VOID

I was scared and alone. I had no idea who I was, or how to fill the emptiness. What would I do on weekends and holidays? I was so scared I could hardly breathe. On weekends I would pace around and have anxiety attacks. My friends all had someone to share their life with.

I threw myself into my job. I could totally immerse myself in my work; success was like a drug. People would get out of training and tell me they had heard so much about me. I would gloat. Humility was defiantly not a problem for me. Managers liked me because I worked really hard and did whatever I was told.

I even took off every Friday afternoon for my massage and never worked in bad weather. It is so good to be at the top. Everything was going to be fine. I had a nice place to live with a lake view, and I was making a lot of money.

I tried all sorts of things to fill up my time. I discovered classes at the local community college.

I took a psychology class. I loved it and had experienced most of what was in the book from all of my years at counseling and living. I could have taught it. I got the highest grade in the class. I took a sculpture class; I pounded on my stone for six weeks and created what I thought was a masterpiece, but my teacher told me I was artistically inhibited. I was crushed. Get it? Rock. Crushed.

I always believed that you could do anything if you really wanted to, so I took a French class. I was wrong. I couldn't do it. Too many *vous*. I took a painting class. No artistic ability there either. I took aerobics but when they went left, I went right. I even tried counseling again. He told me I had worked on all of my issues and was ready to have a healthy relationship. I was willing to try anything. I was learning to be alone. I knew I had to get to know me, make myself happy, and not depend on someone else to make me happy.

I waited for someone to bring me flowers, it didn't happen. I had to start doing things that would nurture my spirit; I could not work and then come home to feel awful. I started buying myself flowers, and even today, you will always see fresh flowers on my table. If I was down, I would go buy myself an ice cream cone. Little things! I had to make an effort, to take care of myself.

I had been to the highest high and the lowest low. I needed to find the middle. What would that take? Little things! Little things, which would add up to big things.

CHAPTER 16
AND MY HEART SMILED...

THE SAD LITTLE GIRL GOES HOME

Ryan, if you have not learned anything yet, please read this.

I had been in AA for seventeen years. Remember the 8th step says we need to make amends. I still had no problem saying "Sorry." I was asked to speak at meetings several times that year. It was always on step eight. Whenever I was asked to speak, I read about that step. The one thing that kept jumping out at me was that "the primary purpose of this step is FORGIVENESS." Forgiveness? I would sooner die with the resentment in my soul towards both moms and my step dad. Even in sobriety, every time I thought about it I had a knot in my stomach. Every time I drank, I drank to kill this pain that they had caused, and I would die with it. I was a victim. I had done no wrong. I was an innocent child.

I had a strong urge to go back to see my foster mom. I had not talked to her for fifteen years. At this time, my own son Jim was actually living in the same town and I could stay with him. I thought while I was there to see him, I should go spend a weekend in my hometown, which was forty miles away. I asked him to go to the beach with me and stay for the weekend. They have great seafood that I never got to have back in Chicago.

There are only two ways to get into town, because it is an island - the causeway, which is a long bridge across the water, or a ferry on the other side of the island. We chose the causeway. As we were driving across, I could taste the salt water on my lips and feel the humidity coming from the gulf. I had never left my hometown until I got married. In my growing up years, I was certain the whole world was eighty-five degrees and sunny every day.

When I left, I didn't think I would ever come back. We were driving down Broadway to get into town. Oleander and date palm trees go down the center of the highway throughout the whole island. It was tropical, and beautiful in its own unique way and quite different from Chicago. I had always missed the beauty of the island but I loved having snow on Christmas. That's probably why I stayed in the Midwest, plus this island was not a haven of happy memories, to begin with.

We were on our way to the beach and we stopped at a light. I hadn't been paying attention, because I was just taking in the beauty of all of the flowers that I had not seen for a long time. As we stopped at the light, I looked to my right and there it was. The house I had lived in from seven until I got married at seventeen. Time was rewinding in my head, like I was there again as a youngster. I could almost see Lillian walking out through the door. The house was still white, with those huge green storm shutters that had to always be closed. It reminded me of something out of a scary movie.

"Wait... stop, park the car," I said. I wanted to go inside. It was now an antique store. I didn't know what to expect. As I walked in, I started shaking.
A lady walked toward me and said, "Can I help you? We have some great things to see."
I had a lump on my throat, but managed to say, "I lived in this house almost all of my childhood, would you mind if I went upstairs?"

"It is mostly storage upstairs," she said.

"I don't mind I won't take long, if that would be OK?" "You can go with me, if you want."

"No it will be fine, take your time."

I went through the door. I was scared. It felt like I was walking into a burning building. There they were the stairs that I would climb every night to safety.

I heard our words.
"Mom can I please have a new bathing suit, because the other one is too small?"
"NO."
"You're not my real mother. My real mother would buy me the bathing suit." I said.
"No I am not. Your mom didn't want you, and I don't either."

I never cared about the abuse; I just wanted a mom's love and no mom wanted me. I grabbed the rail for support and climbed the stairs. What would I find? I got to the top and walked cautiously to the back corner room, not knowing what to expect.

As I got into the room I could hear the yelling.
"You are so useless. Sometimes, I can't stand you."
"Stay in your room, until I tell you to come out."
"Stop crying, or else I will beat you more."
"You used too much water for your bath. Now my bill will be too high."
"Get to work, don't talk, you make me sick when I hear you talk."
"Don't ever let me catch you talking to Lock, or you will be punished."

All of the words were coming rapidly. I needed to get out of there I felt like I would faint.

I thanked the lady and went to the car to be with Jim. "Let's get out of here and go have some fun," I cheered. We had a nice time and good food. I forgot for awhile why I came. I dreaded what was coming.

I now had to do what I came to do, face the lady I had hated all of my life.

LOVE, LILLIAN

I went to see her the next day. There were no big greetings, no hugs, or kisses. This was the woman I thought was my mom, that I hadn't seen her for seventeen years. Neither one of us was glad to see each other.

We didn't talk much, mostly we just sat there. I kept thinking, "Why am I here?" I didn't want to think about the pain this lady had caused me to carry through my life, but I couldn't help it. It all came rushing back. I remembered that she had never hugged me, told me that she loved me, or even had a conversation with me. The only emotion I had shared with her was anger. Her telling me how useless and hopeless I was as a child. She never had an encouraging word. I remembered her tearing up my report card. Not showing up for anything at school. I remembered crashing into the wall when she back handed me and my ears ringing. Then she would hit me until I stopped crying. No Christmas or birthday presents. No holiday dinners. I remembered being scared in my crib, crying for comfort, and her coming in yelling and hitting me for crying.

I had already been with my real mom. Enough was enough. Why was I guided to be here? I went to see her every day for a week. It was all too much to bear. I wanted to go home, where it was safe.

It was time to go, and never to return, or see her again.

It was my last day there, I would say goodbye and wonder why I had even come. I still had the bitterness in my heart and soul. I remember looking at her. For the first time, I could clearly see the pain and sadness in her eyes. Her mom had put her into an orphanage for awhile because she was not able to take care of her. At thirteen, while she was there, she was raped so badly that she could not have children.

She was a beautiful woman. She had been asked to be in a movie and had a contract. Before she was to leave she had an accident that would prevent her from going to Hollywood. She had six husbands, and I think they were in her life to cover up the pain. She outlived all of them and like me, always needed to have a man. She was good with men, and got married for the last time at seventy-five. She never should have had children. She would not even acknowledge that she had grandkids.

I couldn't wait to get out of there. I put my arms around her to kiss her goodbye, without any emotion, thinking it would be the last time.

She put her arms around me, looked into my eyes, and said, "You know, I really loved you, and I did the best I could…"

And like the opening of the shutters from a dark room, the world was suddenly bright. It became absolutely clear to me, she had! She loved me, as much as she knew how. She could not give me something she didn't have. The little love she had, she gave it to me, somehow.

I felt God in the room, and suddenly, all of the pain was lifted from me. I felt it coming out of my body like a cloud. It was a strange feeling, and I had nothing to do with it. But I understood for the first time. I knew I had forgiven her. I loved her for the very first time. I had a miracle. "I love you too." I promised to return soon.

The mother that I never had as a child has finally come into my life... perhaps it was just a matter of figuring out who I am, and what truly matters... forgiveness.

THE LAST SAND CASTLE

I went to the beach, about forty miles away, where I had gone as a child. The tide was out so it was a perfect time to do what I came to do. Build a sand castle. I sat for a long time making the sand castle perfect, with the bridges and moats. It was the most beautiful sand castle I had ever built. This time I did not need a prince to rescue me. God was there. I told God I would stay until he washed the sand castle away. I asked him to take my pain with it.

I sat and waited for the tide, just listening to the waves and reflecting on the miracle that I had just received. As the tide returned, I watched the waves take the sand castle and my pain away. I have never felt that pain again.

UN-LOCKING

My job was not done; I needed to make peace with my step dad, Lock. Lillian married him when I was three, and I had to live with them until I got married. He played a bigger, more important role in my life. One that would destroy every hope I would have to have a healthy relationship with a man. At least Lillian and I had emotion. Lock had abandoned me and left me to suffer. Because he was so weak, he refused to help me when I asked.

I would try to talk to him outside, so my mom wouldn't know we were talking. She was insecure and wanted me to love her more. Plus, she had taken her step dad away from her own mom and married him. I was never allowed to talk to Lock or be alone in the same space. And he allowed it to happen.

I would say, "Daddy, please help me." He would say "Leave me out of it." He never helped me even once. *It gave me a good idea about the graveness of a sin of omission. Sometimes the things that we refuse to do can have bigger consequences than the wrong things that we choose to do.* He would watch her hitting me and punishing me unjustly and walk away. I would never be sure of a man's love or have the skills to have a real relationship. He taught me not to trust that people would help me. He taught me the true meaning of self-sufficiency. It was a good lesson to learn, since I would live alone thirty seven-years of my adult life. It was just a hard lesson to learn at four years old.

I still do not like weak people.

I went to the cemetery where Lock was buried. I had to ask where the grave was because I did not go when he died. It was covered with weeds and I couldn't see his name. I went to a store and bought scissors, cleaner, and a brush. I went back to his grave. I sat for a long time, cutting away the weeds. I then cleaned his stone with cleaner and a brush until it sparkled. When that was done, I told him I forgave him and left. I could move on. And now, my heart can really smile…

* * * * * * * * * *

I had read in the Bible about forgiveness and heard about it in AA, but I had no idea that the pain I was carrying around with me was such a soul sickness. I could not let the good in, until I could get the bad out.

My good friend died with resentment toward her dad for sexual abuse. I understand the unwillingness to forgive the pain that others have caused. She died taking anti-anxiety medication and tranquilizers. She was miserable and in constant emotional and physical pain. The pain could have been gone if she just forgave.

God really did help me forgive because all of my adult life, I could not do it on my own.

152

CHAPTER 17
BREAKING THE CYCLE

Ryan, you come from a family of addicts, and you are the only one that can break the cycle. Do whatever it takes to stop this sickness from going into your family.

Your cousin Lynn is now twenty-four years old. She lived with me for two years because she wanted to be a pediatric neurologist. She quit school a couple of credits short of being a junior to do cocaine, and in three months time became $28,000.00 in debt because of credit cards and student loans that came due because she quit school. She got evicted from her apartment because she was unemployed. She is taking a class this semester and says she wants to be an RN. She was sober one year exactly when she lived with me but says she no longer needs AA.

Sue, her sister, is twenty. She is seven months pregnant by her neighbor and not married. I'm sure she was smoking pot and drinking with her neighbor the night she got pregnant. She got fired from her last two jobs because she says people don't like her. She plans to have welfare help her with the baby. I explained that I had raised two kids without welfare or child support, and she should find a way to care for her child. She accused me of not being supportive.

Your Uncle Jim is now forty-six and divorced for the fourth time. Three of his wives told me they divorced him because of his drinking. He is sleeping on an air mattress in someone's basement and says he will never go to AA again. He went once and stayed for one year. He has lost everything and is starting over. The government is garnering his paycheck for back child support.

Your dad is now forty, Ryan, as I write this book. He was sober the first time for four years. He then drank again for seven years. He has now been sober for twelve years and attends AA meetings regularly. He is the best dad ever and is the only person in my family in recovery.

Your mom was in AA for one year, but she stopped going when you were born. She is now doing prescription drugs

Your seventeen-year-old half brother just got arrested at school for doing drugs, your half sister was diagnosed with an eating disorder. Your mom says she has done drugs also. She is fifteen.

It just keeps going on and on. Please Ryan, do not start. Remember, we can choose our choices, but we cannot choose our consequences. There is no such thing as a little bit in a family of addicts.

It would be grandiose of me to take full responsibility for my family's addiction. Jim was fourteen and Scott was eight when I got sober and I did my very best to show them the way. I gave my granddaughters every opportunity to have a good life. They have made other choices for now. The lesson is that we are powerless over others' choices, and we have to love everyone for who they are, not for who we want them to be. Love will prevail. Love everyone and pray for God's will for their lives. God will always love them and be there in spite of them, just like he was for me.

CHAPTER 18
I LOVE YOU, MOM

LILLIAN

I took care of Lillian for the next fifteen years. The last four years of her life, she needed to be in a home for Alzheimer's. I spent $4,800.00 a month to take care of her and flew down to see her every two months. I really loved her toward the end of her life.

She never acknowledged that I had children, but in her last years, her whole room was full of their pictures that she put up. I have often thought that she was trying to make peace with her past before she died. One day, she said "I love you." It was the only thing she said in three years and I think it was only the second time in her life she told me she loved me.

I had hospice take care of her because she would get more attention when I could not be there. I would have never thought that I would be concerned about her care. She was in hospice for two years because they never knew when she would die. They told me it could be two weeks or two years. There was no way to tell. When I could not be there, they would put the phone by her pillow. I would call and say comforting things to her. This was the lady that had thrown me against the wall, and I still have trouble hearing out of one ear. I had come a long way.

When she died, I flew down. All of her friends had died. Jim, my son, was still living there so he and I were the only ones that attended. I got her a beautiful casket and flowers. I had a minister say prayers, and even rented a tent. I paid for it, so it would be a nice burial for someone that tried her best. She was eighty-six.

It's all about forgiveness. It has made me more loving to everyone. Get the pain out, let the good in.

CLAIRE

My real mom, Claire, was trying really hard to make up for what she has done, or had not done. In fact, I was not being very nice at all. I would come to regret that.

She would ask what I wanted for Christmas. I would ask for something really expensive, even though I knew they didn't have money. She owed me. She would get it and I would feel justified. I insisted she come to my house for Christmas, even though she lived 3,000 miles away. She would come. I went to see her a couple of times but still would not let her get close enough to hurt me again, after that statement. She didn't want me and now I didn't want her. I never thought about the fact that her mom had died at forty-five from alcoholism, and I never heard her talk about a dad. She had her own pain, but all cared about at the time was mine.

I asked her about a will and if she had money to leave anyone. She said she was leaving everything to the church, because they had been her family. I told her she had a new family, MINE! And she should be responsible for them. Until she died, I did not know her decision. One day I got a call from my step dad, Bill. He really liked me, and he adored my Scott. It was the family he always wanted, because Claire could not have kids after me.

He called to say that my mom was in intensive care, on life support. Her intestines had ruptured and her organs were shutting down. I called the hospital and asked them to do whatever it took to keep her alive, until I could get there. I needed to forgive her before she died and I was running out of time.

She was conscious when I arrived. When she saw me, she knew she was dying. I would have never come otherwise and she knew it. She could not speak. I felt bad for her when I saw fear in her eyes. I stood behind her so I would not have to look into her eyes, and I told her I forgave her. I have often thought that I am glad she could not respond, because I could not have handled a discussion.

Her decision was for no life-saving measures, so someone had to make the decision to disconnect her. My step dad couldn't do it. They had been married over fifty years. She was his everything, not having any family.

The decision was mine to make and I thought that was very strange. She brought me into the world and I was taking her out.

I told them to pull the plug.

Bill did not know how to live without her. He was a dear man and I talked to him several times a week to try and comfort him. He treated me like the daughter he never had. I went to see him, but nothing would make him feel better. A year after my mom died, he died too.

I went to bury him, and actually felt worse for his death than my mom's. He had been so much like the father that I never had, even if it was brief. Both had wanted to be scattered at sea, and he had saved her ashes so they would be scattered together. Scott and I chartered a boat and scattered their ashes. Then we went to read the will.

They had left everything to me. I was surprised. She had really tried to please my wishes. It was not a lot but because of this money, I was able to pay off my car and some debt. I could now retire. This one act really helped me, so indirectly; it made up for all of the neglect.

I felt so bad that I had not been nice to my mom. Looking back, she tried so hard but I would not let her get close. She was not the warm fuzzy mom that I wanted. Plus, I didn't trust her. But once again, she too had done her best. I wrote her a letter, telling her how I really felt. I knew it couldn't be mailed but I was sincerely sorry for my behavior and hopefully she knows.

There is no going back, another lesson. Let people know how you feel, so you can work it out. You never know when you will see them again. I do not want to die with regret. Now, that pain would be gone too.

Bill left his computer to Scott. Scott had tried sales but was not performance driven, like I was. I kept trying to get him into customer service because he is so laid back. When we sent the computer home, he took it apart and rebuilt it. This would now be the start of his business, computer repair. He taught himself.

So, Claire and Bill made a real difference in my family's life. Scott would be able to provide for his family and I could retire.

Thanks, Mom.

CHAPTER 19
BECOMING WHOLE

THE PIECES OF MY MOSAIC

I have always thought my life was the mosaic, but a very wise person told me I am the mosaic and I think that is true. I hope we have a lot more pieces to complete the picture.

When God was writing the script for my life, He didn't even consult me. I thought I could be the director, but He said NO. So then I thought I could be the producer and He said not only could I not be the producer, but I couldn't even be the assistant. No matter how much I tried to change the script and make it come out the way I thought it should, I was met with resistance. I have always thought I had a better plan, but He did not cooperate. So I really had no choice but to surrender to His plan, sometimes reluctantly.

THE LAST FIVE YEARS

I retired about five years ago and that was really the beginning of a metamorphosis. Until that time, men had been the focus of my life and then the last twenty-two years, before I retired, I was devoted to my job and success.

I strongly recommend that when you consider retirement, you have a plan, of what you intend to do with your time. I had not given it a thought and was just glad I didn't have to have the stress anymore. Everyone thought I would work until I died, and I never thought I would ever consider retiring. I had made a decision that I would leave only when the job ceased to be fun. When I was getting sick to my stomach going to work, I knew it was time.

I was sixty-one.

Who would have thought that I, with a ninth grade education, would be able to retire with a BMW in the garage and enough money to buy whatever I wanted? I recognize that blessing every day of my life. I am thankful.

THE RETIRED LIFE

The first month was great. I would sit outside and feel the stress leaving my body. Then, it really set in. I went from all of that recognition, people saying "I have heard so much about you," to nothing. I went from everyone wanting my opinion, to no one wanting my opinion. I went from making huge paychecks to earning nothing. I stood in my family room, feeling useless. Now what do I do with my time? I would go everyday to check the calendar to see if something had popped up. I annoyed my friends that were still working with calls. I even asked if they still liked me, and they told me they were talking to me more than ever. It was not enough. I met the mailman at the door because he was the only live person I would see in a day. I had no one to talk to. I went from working over 400 accounts a year and $4,000,000.00 of billing to nothing.

I kept going to the office, because I had nothing to do. Plus, I liked the excitement. I worked a small account because of boredom and made $700 in five minutes. I was hooked. It occurred to me at that time that I am an adrenaline junky. I had never realized it while I was in the midst of the excitement. When you make money or lose money in a short period of time, you get a rush. It is exciting, and I was addicted.

160

They told me, I could call my shots. I could work accounts from home. I would not have to sell new business, which I hated, and could do it any way I wanted. I could choose my accounts. Wow, that sounded perfect, and I could make extra money. I was having a really hard time with not doing anything.

My daughter-in-law, pointed out that I really needed to get used to retirement. If I continued to work accounts, I would eventually have to deal with the nothingness and that I was only prolonging it. She was right. I would have to let go of the excitement.

That was June. I looked at every class at the college but didn't like any of them. I have never been good at sports, so that was out. My mom had the shell store, and I would never touch a craft again.

I needed something, but what? I wanted to make a big difference. I wanted it to be grand.

THE SPIRITUAL PATH

In January of that first year, I was laying on the couch, staring into space wanting to die. I felt that my life had no meaning or purpose.

I had been going to a Christian church with my son Jim and found a book that might help. It said the real purpose for our lives was to help people by doing little things. Little things? I wanted grand!!! I wanted to make a big difference.

It talked about David and Goliath and how during WW II they dropped gum behind the lines for the kids, and how much of a difference a little piece of gum made in a child's life.

I was already doing little things, making chicken soup for my sick neighbors, giving rides, running errands, staying with my friends after surgery, and just being available to help where needed.

I investigated volunteering. One thing about volunteering, you can leave anytime and show up when you want. It does not require a big commitment, unless you want to.

I tried working with abused women, but it raised too many issues for me and I could not do it. Then, I found a volunteer job that raised money to help abused women and children. I needed indirect involvement.

One of the organizations that we helped invited me to a benefit. When I got there they told me that I was the guest of honor. I did not understand and felt undeserving. I no longer wanted to be the star. I wanted to be in the background. I no longer needed recognition. I preferred to be anonymous.

I noticed that I was getting nicer. I was so consumed with my job; I did not have the time or energy to pay attention to my surroundings. I took people in stores that were helping me for granted. Wasn't it their job to serve me?

Now with time on my hands, I noticed people. I sincerely began to appreciate the help they were giving me. I would ask them how they were doing before they asked me. Some of them were surprised that anyone noticed them, at all.

I volunteer at the food bank. It is very humbling and makes me so grateful that I can buy whatever I want to eat. These people have nothing. I am always grateful for the ability to buy food. The days of Kool-Aid and bologna really made a difference. When I work at the food bank, I understand, but they don't know it. I too, was without money or food to eat.

THE CATHOLIC GOD

I volunteered to help John, the director of the food bank, organize his office. He had gone to seminary to be a monk. He started talking to me about going back to Catholic Church. I told him I would sooner die. That God was the punishing God.

I had now been sober thirty-three years. I had a Higher Power which was God, and I was attending the Christian church. I have been baptized Catholic, Lutheran, Baptist, and Christian. I was married to an Episcopal and a Methodist. I was covered. No need to go through that again. That Catholic God had let me down.

Every time I was at the food bank, John would talk to me about going back to Catholic Church. To appease him I thought I would try it just once and then tell him that I didn't like it.

I had heard about a priest, Father Michael, that had come to the community two years ago and everyone said he was amazing. I thought I would try and see if that was true. Then I would not have to go back. It had been forty years since I had been in a Catholic Church. He was not there for the mass, but just going through the mass and sitting in the church gave me comfort. It was familiar. When the mass was over and I was leaving, Father Mike, the priest I wanted to see, was sitting outside the chapel. He had no reason to be there, no appointments and it was his day off. I know that God put him there for me. I told him how resistant I was to coming back. We talked for two hours and laughed most of the time.

I told him about my God Can and that I had made it out of a coffee can. I pasted a label to the can and cut a hole in the top. When I have a problem, I write the problem down on a piece of paper and put that in the God Can. It gets it out of my head, and into the can. "I can't, but GOD CAN." I check it about every six months and so far nothing that I have put into it has changed, but it is the practice of letting go.

Father Mike suggested that we get together and talk and I agreed. There was something different about him, not like the priest that I knew forty years ago. The day we were supposed to meet, he had an emergency and asked if he could stop by my house later. Sure, I didn't know priest made house calls. He showed up with a cake, took off his shoes, and got comfortable on the couch. He talked to me about his own pain in life. He was a real person, not the image that I always had of a priest. It was a profound experience and because of his "realness," I decided to try going to church again. They were right, he is amazing and I would not have even given it a thought if it had not been for him. God knew what would get through to me.

* * * * * * * * * *

For the last five years, I had been attending a Christian church, but it was not the same for me. The peace that I have experienced going back to the Catholic Church is like nothing I have experienced before. The Catholic Church was my only source of comfort when I was going through the pain of my childhood, but I left because of what I was taught at the time about the punishing God. But the punishing God has died in my life, while the loving, merciful God now lives forever.

I was born with innocence and pure love from God. Then, I had many negative experiences. I spent the rest of my life trying to get back to that place of innocence in my heart and soul. It feels like I am finally home. I have completed the circle.

It has made me more aware of my powerlessness and my willingness to turn my family over to God's hands. He never let me go. His grace was there, even when I was at my worst. He helped me in spite of myself. When I wanted to die, He saved me, because He had a mission for me.

I know today that all of my experiences of child abuse, domestic violence, alcoholism, family, losing a child, divorce, and trying a job were possible because of God's grace. I have experienced a lot. I know that God wants me to use those experiences to help others get through their lives.

Being alone in your own head is like being in a bad neighborhood all by yourself. We need God's guidance and advice from our friends.

Today, I am a good, loving, caring person that has grown out of pain. To the degree that you have experienced pain, you can experience joy. Today I am joyful. Yes, I am alone at home but it occurred to me that if I had a man in my life, I wouldn't have been able to help as many people as I do. Would I be willing to help, or would I be totally devoted to taking care of my man? God knows what's best for me.

The real key in my life is acceptance. Acceptance that things are the way they are supposed to be. I have been molded and God has the master plan. His decisions for my life have always been the best. I am not capable of making good choices, on my own.

TRUE FRIENDS

This birthday was wonderful. It was scary for me, because no one has ever remembered my birthday. I have only had two cakes in my life: one when I was twelve and one I bought for myself.

Friends brought me cakes, bouquets of flowers, and wonderful cards. Five people told me they were better people because of me. Three people told me I was a blessing in their lives. Two people told me I was special.

"Are you talking about me?" Who is that person and where did she come from?! It made me feel so good, but those old tapes said, "Don't believe them. They must be talking about someone else." Sometimes I have trouble seeing that I am an asset. I just do what I am guided to do and still have a hard time accepting affirmations. When I came to AA, I had never had a friend and had no idea how wonderful it is to have someone who cares.

The only time I could see that I was making a difference was in my work with my customers. I knew I was doing a good job because I cared.

On a personal level, I feel uncomfortable. I wish I could believe the nice things people say about me all of the time. It's a brand new experience.

I have a bible study at my house every week with my neighbors. It has been a great experience because we have bonded and are always available to each other for care and support. I am blessed to have such wonderful neighbors. This will be our sixth year together.

CRYING IN GRATITUDE

That's the whole story. Just imagine. These were only the highlights, but I have told everything that mattered, everything that I thought was significant in making me into the person I am today.

I am in awe of God's plan for my life. My life has been so very blessed. Today I realize that I have everything I need and everything that I have asked for. I have prayed all of my life for someone to really love me. I thought it would be a man, because I asked for someone to share my life with. But I have been blessed with wonderful friends, friends that really love me. It makes me cry with gratitude. He answered my prayers because I never gave up believing. It turned out better than I ever thought possible.

Looking back at my whole life, I wondered, "Who was that other person?" Who was that little girl that got beat for crying? Who was that little girl that built sand castles on the beach, hoping that a prince would come and rescue her from the abuse? Who was that girl that got married at seventeen, hoping for a better life? Who was that woman that had her nose broken and saw her blood all over the wall? Who was that woman that lay dying on a bed in intensive care, not wanting to die, but not knowing how to live? Who was that woman that was shaking at her first AA meeting, not wanting to belong, but was there because she wanted to kill her kids the night before? Who was that woman that found the courage to leave the job at the dentist and go into sales, with no skills or education?

It was ME!!! I am here! The new improved version! Someone real, someone you know...

* * * * * * * * *

Writing this book has been one of the most painful, difficult thing I have done in my life. It has made me nauseous, given me backaches, and made me cry a lot. I had to relive everything that I had shoved down or rationalized away. But this was real therapy. I had to revisit everything one more time, so I could heal completely. Because I can now go back to my memories of the pains that I went through, I know that I am no longer afraid and I can really be who I am. Although the painful memories remain painful when I remember them, I am no longer subjected to the oppression that the past gave me. I am freed by forgiveness, by understanding that there is a meaning and purpose even for my pains and that God loves me. It is awesome!

And when something beautiful and wonderful is given to me, I cannot help but share it and point it out to everyone so they too can see it. I guess, ultimately, that is why I am writing this book. I want to share my blessings. Now everyone can know the REAL me. I hope my story can help someone get to the other side and get unstuck. No one should have to endure the kind of pain that I experienced, but there is hope.

But my most important reader is you, Ryan, because I want you to know how much I love you and how much more God loves you, even when it may be hard to see it sometimes.

Ryan, I taught you to say the Rosary. It protected me and it will protect you too. Remember the times we laid in bed and said our rosary? Ryan, I always thought you should be a priest. If you are not called to be one, it does not matter. You have so much to offer the world; God has blessed you and made you special. Use your love and caring spirit to help others, no matter what vocation you receive from God. The time we were together was so special to me. I could pour out all of the love I stored up for all of my life into you. I could not have asked for a better ending to the story. Or is it the beginning? I am now whole.

I was looking at the cemetery behind my house, where someday I will be buried. I was wondering if some of my pain and suffering and the quality of my life the last thirty years has earned me a place in heaven.

If it did, I will ask God for a special favor. I will ask Him if He will let me be your guardian angel so I can guide you, protect you, and help you to make good choices for your life. Remember Ryan, when you say you're Guardian Angel Prayer, which I taught you, you could be talking to me. I hope so. I will always be in your heart and I will NEVER let you down or stop loving you.

Just like God!

* * * * * * * * * *

So, this story ends. I will continue to love you until the last day of my life, but will love you even more in the next life! As you close the final pages of this little book, I hope you realize that I have told you everything I learned about living. Sometimes, alone in my garden where you usually play in the afternoon when you come to visit me, I watch the birds that visit in the shade of the trees. I think of the mother birds feeding their little ones in their nests. They never tire to fly around or to look for something to feed their young. Then, in the proper season, the young little birds have to grow and fly out of their mother's nests.

Ryan, I am confident that you are ready to fly and soar into the heights. Always carry my love in your heart.

Fly away, little bird…

EPILOGUE
LESSONS FOR LIVING

Ryan, these ones are all for you. I have a feeling that these are going to be the most important things that I can leave behind for you to carry with you for the rest of your life. There might even be a time when you will not remember exactly all the things that we have shared and, perhaps, you will even vaguely remember my own face. But I leave you these important gifts, and I pray that they will always be clear forever.

THE ART OF CARING

For so many years, I was not capable of loving anyone because of my mistrust. No one would get close to my heart. It was emotional aloofness. After years of therapy, AA, and some efforts on my part, I began healing because of the forgiveness. I was willing to love and be loved. I became aware of people and how to respond and give. All of the emotion that I had shoved down, far away, would now be able to resurface.

It took me a long time to establish a value system in my life. I was never taught any values when I was growing up. I went to a counselor once, after I got sober. He said, "What are your values?" I asked, "What's a value?"

Today, I can actually feel someone else's pain. I cannot stand to see anything hurt or suffer. I have trouble visiting hospitals and could never work in one. Even if I find a bug in my house, I catch it and take it outside. I caught a mouse in my basement. Its foot was caught. I told him to stay still and I would let him go outside. He stayed still. He is probably back in my basement but I guess everyone needs a home. We are all God's creatures.

I was working so hard and had never paid attention to how to treat people. I had to learn from others how to do it. I was empty and what I took for granted had been taught from my childhood. I had no role models ever. Life from the time I was born was that I needed to be self-sufficient and take care of myself. I learned everything by observation. All of the skills that someone would have normally, I had to teach myself.

I remember sitting next to someone at work and they said, "Thank you for calling." I thought that was a strange thing to say. I had never really made an effort to be polite. I had always taken people for granted and never really noticed my surroundings. I started doing it until it felt natural.

I asked my friend why she didn't call me and she asked me how often I called her? I hadn't. I was always waiting for someone to call me.

So now I call. In order to have a friend, you have to be a friend.

ON PASSING JUDGMENTS

When I was in Mexico, it rained the whole time. Oprah was on with a show about passing judgment. It said that every time we pass judgment, even if it is while we are driving, it causes us pain. It can create chronic back pain and headaches. The person you are judging or yelling at, while you are driving, don't know it. It is just hurting you. What right do we have to play God? We do not know what is going on with that person.

I really listened to this. I was arrogant and I did feel better than some people at work because I was at the top. I was defiantly passing judgment on a person at work. I decided to practice on her.

Every time I saw her, I would think, "You are so stupid." I was sure if I could stop judging her, I could stop judging others. I really did not like her at all and wondered how she ever got the job, even though she had a master's degree and I went to ninth grade.

I made up my mind to go blank when I talked to her. I would not allow myself to think any thoughts. It took awhile but I noticed I was starting to like her. Since that lesson, I have tried not to pass judgment on anyone. I cannot pretend to be better or know what is going on with someone else.

ON PREJUDICE

Another lesson that God has given me is about prejudice. I had no prejudice, except for Indian people. I lived by a lady that was really dirty with dirty diapers lying on the floor of her apartment above mine. It was making my apartment stink. Another was a customer that was my worst to deal with. She always accused me of being dishonest and would have me come back five times. She would stand me up and treat me badly. My conclusion was that I didn't like this nationality, and I assumed they were all alike.

One day I heard about a lady whose husband set her kids on fire. I went around to my neighbors to collect money for her because she couldn't work. Her husband was in jail, and her children were in the hospital. She had to stay at the hospital twenty-four hours a day. I collected $2,500 for her, even though I had never met her. I called the hospital and even got to talk to her. I told her I wanted to set up an account for her at a bank, and she needed to go to the bank to sign the papers. I had already contacted a lawyer to do this. She agreed to do it. I called all of the newspapers and TV stations. The story went international because of the newspapers. People from India were calling me to see how they could contribute.

I still had not met her at this point, but I knew she was Indian. When I met her, my heart broke for her. I continued to raise money for her and she invited me to both her son's funerals. In one moment she lost her sons, house, job (from staying at the hospital), and her husband. There is always someone worse off.

Thank you, God, for this lesson. I no longer have any prejudice.

ON BEING HONEST

Another time, I was working a big account that spent over $300,000.00 a year. They did not know what they had. They told me to do whatever I thought was best and would not see what they had for eighteen months since it was advertising. I needed money. I could put anything in and they would never know because the bill was paid in Holland. I was shocked and ashamed by what I thought and realized I would never be immune to dishonesty.

I needed to pay attention and always try and live the way God wanted or else I would have guilt and might drink. Nothing would be worth that, but it was my first awareness of the temptation to be dishonest. We have to live with the consequences, no one is immune.

Always be honest in everything you do. God will reward you.

ON TITHING

Probably one of the most significant lessons I learned is about tithing my money. I had been attending a Christian church and the sermon was on tithing money.

They said we should give 10% to the church. At that time, I was making $170,000.00. (Can you believe that? I am still amazed). Wait a minute. That would be $17,000.00 you want me to give. I thought, "That's too much. I can't afford it." I came home and read the bible. I found nine passages about giving and helping others. I am biblically impaired so I'm sure there are more references. It said we should use our money to help the poor and sick and God would reward us. It says all of our needs will be met if we do this.

I had never thought about that. I was too self-absorbed and afraid that I needed to keep my money for retirement. I made a deal between me and God. I figured if I didn't see some reward, I could always go back to my $5.00 a week. I told no one.

The following day, I had been thinking about retiring. I had not checked my retirement account for a couple of years. The amount had doubled and I could retire anytime I wanted. I would have enough to live on for life, without having to work again. I was sixty-one.

I would continue to give to help others. When you are retired, you are in a very tenuous place. Should you spend your money and enjoy it, or should you save it in case you need it for healthcare? I give my money faithfully, and with faith, to help others. Sometimes I think I am not going to have enough, but it always works out in the most unusual ways. Workers come and work for me. They give me discounts or don't charge me at all. People send me refunds that I didn't expect. There is always enough. God gave me the ability to make the money. I am just following the instructions in the Book. If you don't have enough, you're not giving enough.

ON NEVER GIVING UP

Ryan, all of your life you will face challenges and hard things that may seem impossible. Try. Do not quit. Keep trying! You will never succeed at anything if you give up. Remember how much I believed in you about catching the ball, or the mind games. You will have bosses that don't like you and you may not like them, but that is no reason to quit your job. Make it work. Smile and say, "You can count on me. I'm doing the best I can!" Then do it. Ask them to help you. When your cousin was failing and needed to make an "A," I told her to go to the teacher and ask how to do that with six weeks to go. She made an "A," because she asked for help. Don't ever think you're a failure. Anything is possible. YOU can do whatever you want. You have the power. Everything in your life and how it turns out will be based on your choices and perseverance. I have showed you how to be a success. JUST DO IT!

ON WORDS AND CREDIT RATINGS

Ryan I'm sorry to tell you there are only two things in life you can control: your word and your credit rating. This is very important. Always do what you say you are going to do. Never let anyone down. You always knew if I said it, I meant it. Keep your word to your kids and everyone else. People need to know they can count on you to do what you say. Even when I was poor, I managed what I had and have never been one day late on anything. If we can manage our finances, we can manage our lives. Save. You will always need something to fall back on. I always had three months of savings in a different bank.

ON NURTURING RELATIONSHIPS

Ryan, you summed up in five seconds what relationships are all about. You played a learning game all by yourself without needing my help. Then, you went to take a bath, for the first time you told me that you could do it by yourself. Then you got dressed all by yourself. I looked at you with sadness and said, "Ryan, you don't need me anymore."

Without thinking about it, you said, "I need you... I need you to love me, play with me, and cook for me." You told me that three more times that night just to reassure me. Those three things are the most important ways to nurture a relationship. Loving, playing, and sharing a meal. You were five, and you already knew.

ALWAYS ASK FOR HELP

Ask for what you need or want. Don't be afraid. Ask for the manager or the person in charge and ask them to help you. 99% of people will help you. If you ask, people will see that you are standing up for yourself and what you believe in. Even if people tell you, "It will never work," do it anyway. All they can say is "No."

ON KNOWING WHEN TO STOP TALKING
... ☺

POSTSCRIPT

One year later……

Thanksgiving came again, but this time the family was smaller. Jim's divorce was final, so it was just Jim and Lynn. We only talked about superficial stuff as to not create any problems. We ate as soon as dinner was ready. They left immediately to go to a more pleasant environment. We were invited to your house Ryan, but we decided our dysfunctional house was better than yours.

Sue my granddaughter in Oklahoma had her baby last July and is still living with her mom. Grandpa died. Sue has not tried to collect child support from the father; she thinks public aid is better. I offered to pay for college to provide a better future for her and my great grandson but she said no. She still thinks I am not supportive enough.

In November, Jim asks me to give him money for the room he was renting because he said business would be bad until after the first of the year. He told me he was finally going to get sober, and was attending AA every day. I gave him money for November and December to cover rent, car insurance and cell phone. I was so excited to hear he was trying to get his life straightened out.

In January, I left with Father Mike to donate a roof for his church. I asked Jim to stay at my house for my cat and dog. When I called to see how things were going he said he had moved in. Jim and I have not had a good relationship for all of his adult life, because of his drinking, but he told me he was getting sober and had never been more at peace. He wanted to sleep on an air mattress in the basement. I thought that was odd since I have three bedrooms, but I felt that God had given me a chance to finally have a better relationship with him.

In February Scott, your father, told me he wanted a divorce and he wanted custody of you to be able to provide a healthy environment for you. Getting custody would be very expensive, because the court always favors the mom regardless of circumstances. I told him I would help, but I had to borrow money against my house to loan him the money.

Scott left his wife and moved in with you. I am now 66 with both sons back home. I never thought that would happen, but I was OK with it.

About a week into everyone being here, I asked Jim how his day was. He swore at me and told me it was none of my business, and then told me maybe he should move. I didn't say a word. He left and never did come back to live with me after that day. The following month he got a DUI, and lost his license. He is now riding a bike. I see him occasionally on the bike and it breaks my heart. I do not know where he lives, or how he can take care of his business on a bike.

Lynn is working and going to school. She has really progressed and is making A's in all of her classes. She has resentment in her heart for her dad, Jim, but refuses to even think about forgiveness. I explained that carrying the pain around would cause her great harm and that is why she drinks. I told her to get into AA again before she destroys her life trying to cover up the pain, but typically she thinks it will not happen to her.

This is my family; it just goes on and on. Just like Thanksgiving, I always expect it is going to be the happy, loving family that I have always wanted. Sometimes, I get depressed and feel that I am a failure... that somehow I failed in the most important job that God gave me. I have to remind myself that they are all adults, and the choices that they are making do not have much to do with me anymore. I still can't help wishing it were different.

The divorce is still progressing and it is taking a toll especially on you, and everyone. I hope it ends soon, because it breaks my heart to see you suffering because of it.

Scott got a townhouse close to me so I get to see you more often. I pray I can make a positive impact in your life, you will grow up happy, and have a wonderful life. You are the only one that can break the cycle of addiction in our family. Please do this so you can have a marvelous successful future. I am so sorry you have to go through this, and someday you will understand why this all happened. I know this hurts you and you are sad, but the environment that you were in was not a good place.

If it were not for my renewed faith, the Catholic Church, Father Mike and my rosary that is always under my pillow, all of which provide comfort when I can't sleep worrying about my family. I try and share the blessings God has given me by helping others. God has blessed me more than I ever thought possible, and for that I am grateful.

Oh, and the man behind the big red doors, he got blown up by the mob, on a golf course in Florida…….. Justice!